The Psychological Edge In Rugby

Leadership and Motivation in Coaching Team Sports

Michael Gourley

Michael Gourley has a background in industrial and sport psychology. He is a director of Human Synergistics, an international research and management consulting company. This role has given him extensive experience in motivation and leadership in commercial organisations. As a rugby player he was a member of the Victoria University Rugby Club and played for New Zealand Universities. He was also in the squad of the Wellington Provincial team. Besides coaching himself, he has helped coaches understand sport psychology on an individual basis and by conducting coach-the-coaches seminars. He regularly addresses management conferences on achievement motivation. The material he has developed on coaching has been used in New Zealand, Australia, USA and Britain.

The Psychological Edge In Rugby

Leadership and Motivation in Coaching Team Sports

Michael Gourley

Published by Human Synergistics NZ Ltd 2003

Designed and typeset by Egan-Reid Ltd, Auckland
Printed in New Zealand

ISBN 0 473 09388 X

Table of Contents

Dedication

To my mother, who encouraged in me many of the positive attitudes mentioned in this book. I told her that if I wrote a book on rugby I would dedicate it to her for all the dirty gear she washed. Also to my father who was a great supporter on the sideline.

PREFACE

The initial ideas for this book came from the experience of standing in front of St Paul's College first XV, my old school, who had just been promoted to the A division in Auckland secondary schools rugby. They had lost their first game in the new division and were looking to avoid relegation. I had watched their previous game, which was an uninspired effort. Their attitude and spirit completely changed from the first encounter I had with them. From that beginning the team won the championship and went on to win three in a row, and reached a level of performance seldom seen in schoolboy rugby.

The ideas that evolved during that period and subsequent coaching form the basis of this book. I was involved in coaching at senior level and assisting with teams in secondary schools, as well as coaching my own children in junior grades. Of particular mention is John, my brother, who is a teacher, and who had an incredible ability to recognise the merit of what I was saying and helped refine and transform the ideas into coaching principles. Such coaching has brought out the finest qualities in players and the results in championship rounds attest to its effectiveness. Many of these top results have been gained through co-coaching and assisting coaches to understand the motivational principles underlying high performance. These concepts apply over a cross section of teams from junior to senior levels. They can obviously be adapted for the level of competence and maturity of the players concerned.

Initially the reasons behind the success of these ideas were not particularly clear. I was relying on an intuitive understanding of motivation and team dynamics. Subsequently I have been able to reflect on and better articulate the principles of high achievement motivation. Much of this has been made possible through my work in industrial psychology. In my work I have formed life long friendships with Dr Clay Lafferty and Dr Rob Cooke in the US, two outstanding researchers in this field. They are part of Human Synergistics International, a research and management consulting company of which I am a director. Their work and the findings of Professor McClelland on achievement motivation provided insight into the intuitive understanding I had earlier gained from coaching. Our theories are based on the psychological data we have gathered on 35,000 leaders and managers in New Zealand and Australia and over two million others worldwide.

I express appreciation to my colleagues in Human Synergistics in New Zealand and Australia, Shuan McCarthy and Quentin Jones, who have encouraged me in the development of material about coaching and have helped me take the step to publish this book. It is part of a series of publications Human Synergistics has made on psychology, but the first applying our research to sport. I would also like to mention Ken Stead, Maurice Cervin, John Lovell, Brent Anderson and Bruce Gemmell whose help and support were valuable.

While this book analyses and reviews top coaches and international teams it is primarily designed to help club and secondary school coaches motivate their teams to excel. It will help them tap the potential of players in a way that they may have never experienced before. It will however require a little more understanding of human motivation and team dynamics than the usual coaching book. It is only by getting a better appreciation of these concepts that significant gains can be made in getting the right psychological edge for top performance. It is the difference between knowing which note to play on the piano and understanding the music. When this is achieved, coaches discover a new dimension that transforms their team's performance and provides them with some of the most worthwhile experiences they will have in sport.

Part of the reason for writing this book was to support and

encourage coaches to use sport as an important means for teaching players how to face the challenges of life. The values people can learn on the sports field can stand them in good stead in their careers and other endeavours. There is a fine line between sport psychology and industrial psychology, as both are about responding to challenge and developing achievement motivation. This is why there is a lot of rapport between those in sport and commerce. It is for this reason that sportsmen and sportswomen often address company conferences to describe the drive and satisfaction of working hard and achieving goals. In some ways I am doing it the other way around by addressing coaches and sports men and women on motivation and leadership from my business experience.

Chapter 1

THE PSYCHOLOGICAL EDGE

Motivation is the most important aspect of coaching. It is vital – it gives teams a psychological edge. That edge results in superior performance and a determination to win. Ask any top coach what accounts for his or her success and the answer is the ability to motivate players. The legendary American football coach Vince Lombardi said, 'Coaches who can outline plays on a blackboard are a dime-a-dozen. The ones who win get inside their players and motivate.' Graham Henry endorses this: 'Attitude was everything. If the attitude was right we would generally play to a high standard and win.'[1] Yet books on coaching give very little attention to how to gain the psychological edge. Surely, if motivation is what makes the difference, the focus of coaching should be on outlining how to get the best out of players. Instead, these books are full of anecdotes about matches and players, and coaching information on skills, organisation and the technical aspects of the game.

It is not that coaches just pay lip service to motivation; they have a profound belief in the importance of this issue. The problem arises when they try to explain what it is that they do to motivate players. Often they understand intuitively what is required but are unable to explain in words what they mean. When they try to explain what they do to motivate players, they sound tough, hard and uncaring. That is the image of the 'authoritarian' coach, which is a stereotype we still have. However, the most successful coaches are supportive and encouraging. This concern for players is rarely portrayed in the media. Such an inaccurate portrayal can influence others to take an authoritarian approach that is detrimental to the performance of their team.

Take the slogan 'No mistake rugby'. This has become a catch-phrase. However, it doesn't stand up to scrutiny. Rugby has the most complicated rules of any game. It requires a greater range of skills than any other sport and it has the largest number of players making up a team except for Australian Rules football. Put all that together and then say 'No mistakes!' That is setting a standard that denies reality. Focusing on mistakes inhibits performance. Players can avoid making mistakes by not taking risks or chances in the game. Yet the game relies on reflexes, quick judgement and calculated risks.

Let us examine the usual rugby commentary panel on television. In reviewing a game they focus on mistakes. Listening to some of their comments, you would think that the only way a team could score a try was through a mistake made by the opposition. In fact, many of the values they unconsciously advocate run counter to a psychologically constructive approach to sport. It is not that they deliberately set aside consideration of what creates excellence. They are acting out of a lack of understanding and espousing things that are actually detrimental to motivation. Take, for example, the blame that is often associated with losing. The fear of failure is one of the characteristics that undermines and inhibits the drive for achievement.

In contrast, the legendary basketball coach John Wooden, who has been enormously successful at the University of California in Los Angeles, had a saying 'The team that makes the most mistakes will probably win.' There is much truth in that statement if you analyse it properly. He believed that 'The doer makes mistakes, and I wanted doers on my team – players who made things happen.'[2]

Wooden's statement is the complete antithesis of 'No mistake rugby.' From a sport psychology perspective he is completely right. Concentrating on mistakes does not help create excellence. Excellence is achieved by concentrating on positive aspects of performance rather than on negativity. While many of our top coaches are espousing 'No mistake rugby,' often it isn't exactly what they mean. Usually they are more pro-active in fostering excellence. This is where following what they say would have an adverse effect on a team. What they say and what they do are often two different things. If, however, they are unable to articulate what it is that they do to motivate players, how are we to develop other coaches?

Individual versus team psychology

In recent years many books have emerged that discuss sport psychology. While they talk about the principles of motivation, they rarely integrate theory with practice. They tend to remain academic, and the emphasis is on psychological techniques. Often these techniques are more suited to an Olympic athlete than a rugby player. They concentrate on the psychology of the individual and peak performance. A lot of research has been done in this area of sport psychology. This tends to be more relevant to individual players at the top level. For most coaches though, the most important aspect of sport psychology is team motivation. This involves issues such as leadership, dealing with the various personalities in a team and group dynamics. Individual motivation fits within this context.

It is not that skill and strategies are insignificant, but there is often too much concentration on this aspect of coaching and not enough attention to the importance of motivation. Teaching the skills of the game is a starting point in coaching. As players develop, teamwork has more influence and strategy plays an increasing part in the team's performance. It all has to be harnessed to an overall team pattern. Yet underlying all this is the influence of motivation. In many ways, motivation is conveyed through the approach the coach takes to developing skills and strategies. Most coaches do not understand how they convey beliefs and values through the process of developing the skills and strategies that build teamwork and motivation in players.

At the top level, there is a very small gap between success and failure. Often it is motivation that makes the difference. Striking the right motivational balance is the art of effective coaching. This can only be achieved by having a thorough understanding of the motivations that create excellence in individuals and teams. There are certain attitudes, beliefs and values that underlie excellence. It is here that the clues to successful coaching lie. These motivations, or ways of thinking, are associated with effectiveness in sport as well as in business and life in general. This is why lessons learned on the sports field help in other aspects of our lives.

Knowing how players think will tell a lot about their ability to perform. Being able to positively influence and develop their attitudes toward excellence will make an enormous difference in the way they play rugby. Excellence has to do with high achievement values. These values can be defined, they can be measured and they can be developed in individuals and teams. Fostering these values is the most powerful influence a coach can have on a team. It is a key aspect of sport psychology. At this stage it is sufficient to signal that there are important attitudes, beliefs and values that underlie effective performance. In the next chapter we will examine achievement motivation in depth.

Evaluating a rugby game

Coaches must take an overall view of how to develop a psychological edge and how to approach and interpret the game. What is it that you should look for in evaluating a game of rugby? How do you judge how play is going? Is it the score? That can tell you a certain amount, but how often has a team come from behind to win? The score is an indicator but does not really give sufficient insight unless the team is winning by a substantial margin. Is it territorial advantage? Once again, I have seen teams where the territorial advantage was in favour of the opposition, yet they were able to win handsomely. If the score and territorial advantage is not getting at the heart of evaluating a game, then what is? Is it possession? Once again, an analysis can show that the team with the minority of possession can win! Does it come down to the size or apparent skill of the respective teams? Teamwork can overcome superior opposition, so that does not hold up as a way of making an evaluation. Is it the team that makes the fewest mistakes? We have already covered how the doers make mistakes, and to win you need doers!

It can be argued that all these elements play a part in evaluating how the game is going. While there is some truth in this, examining all these elements does not give a very succinct or necessarily accurate picture of how a team is doing. It doesn't provide a clear focus on what the team is trying to achieve. Besides, there is a better way to evaluate a game. These previous definitions rely too much on analysing skills and strategy. They do not take into account the psychological element, which has a big bearing on the outcome and needs to be used in analysing a game. These other criteria have limitations. There needs to be a clear way of appreciating the flow of a game and being able to communicate this to players.

This is where the psychological aspects of the game come into account. I discovered this when playing for Victoria University. We had a strong team but in many games the score was still rather close in the second half and we didn't seem to be making much impression. A game would suddenly seem to open up for us to score. After that, play would get back to being fairly even. It was as if the opposition let us run in tries because they expected us to win; so it happened. It seemed they intuitively accepted that the outcome of the game would be a win to us. As a result it was a self-fulfilling prophesy.

The same phenomenon can happen when two stags challenge each other. It can be seen on television, when two males are head-butting over territory or control of the herd. There does not seem to be any difference as they crash into each other, yet they somehow work out who has the ascendancy. One eventually shows some sign of submission and after a few more exchanges departs. In many ways, sport has elements of that behaviour. When I coached teams that never showed psychological submission, it led to the other team taking the submissive role. We often won in the last stage of the game because they succumbed to our indomitable spirit.

It is this psychological dimension that makes all the difference. It is a quality every player needs to possess. Certainly, it is more evident in successful teams but it is not exclusive to them. Understanding this influence is the start of developing a real appreciation of motivation. The influences are not easily understood. I have worked with coaches who on the surface seemed to understand motivation, but later, after having been successful with teams we jointly coached, were unable to transfer this knowledge to other teams. On the other hand, there were those who were able to pick up the ideas and use them effectively.

There are competing motives and values in a team, some of which can be spurious in motivating top performance, yet many coaches readily subscribe to those values. On the surface, competitiveness may appear to work. It is easy to maintain a competitive style of coaching without being aware of the negative impact it can have if you do not understand the attitudes, beliefs and values that create excellence. This book may challenge some of your assumptions and could require you to change some beliefs you hold. Some people may have a negative reaction to information that is contrary to their view, particularly if it questions some deeply held beliefs about the way they coach. The reaction is usually criticism or lack of acceptance of the information. For example, some coaches are power types and this behaviour will be shown to be a less effective style of operating. They will tend to defend their position and put down other ideas.

The initiative

In evaluating a game of rugby, I have found that the best criterion is to judge which team has the initiative. Focusing on who has the initiative in evaluating how the game is going can provide a significant insight into the likely outcome of the match. Winning often depends on having the psychological balance in your favour. The initiative includes criteria such as possession, territorial advantage and other things discussed above, but it is more than the sum of those technical aspects of the game. The team with the initiative invariably takes the game to the opposition. They initiate and determine the pattern of play, and the opposition follows. This is exactly what the word 'initiative' suggests. Having the initiative enables players to act with confidence and dictate play. It gives them the psychological advantage that invariably leads to winning.

Examples of teams or individuals having the initiative and winning can be found in every sport. In the America's Cup, once a yacht gains the lead it can dictate the tactics to the other. It can take the most favourable side of the course, therefore forcing the opponent into less favourable air. In return the opponent can initiate a tacking duel to try to wrestle the initiative back. The lead boat, however, largely has the initiative.

When Muhammad Ali fought George Foreman for the heavy-weight boxing crown in the 'Rumble in the Jungle,' he seemed to have capitulated early in the fight. The film 'When We Were Kings,' an award-winning documentary on the fight, showed Ali covering his head with his gloves and leaning back against the ropes. It seemed as if he had no answer to Foreman's attack. Although it didn't look it at the time, Ali actually had the initiative – he was fighting the way he wanted the early rounds to go with his 'rope-a-dope' strategy. He took heavy blows to the body and protected his head, even taunting Foreman that he couldn't hit hard enough. He allowed Foreman to wear himself out in the heat and humidity. It took such a toll on Foreman that by the middle of the fifth round he had used up a great deal of his strength. At that point Ali came off the ropes and started to land punches. He knocked Foreman out in the eighth round.

It was a clear case of Ali having the initiative. He had properly assessed his rival and worked out a game plan to deal with his strengths and weaknesses. He knew that he could not match Foreman's power so he concluded he would have to outlast him. While it initially looked odd with Ali leaning back across the ropes, one commentator saying it was like a man leaning out of a window to see what was on his roof, he actually had the initiative. Normally a boxer will never go to the ropes unless he is hurt and trying to defend himself. Foreman had expected Ali to 'dance' and was unprepared for the tactics he used. It was one of the great heavy-weight boxing upsets.

Historically, the All Blacks have often been able to maintain the initiative through the strength of their forwards. More recently, the changes in the rucking laws have reduced their opportunities to gain dominance using this strategy. Domination by the forwards allowed the backs to dictate the tactics and play to the game plan they wanted. It was almost an impossible pattern to break and led to New Zealand success in rugby for decades. There was always a confidence and purpose in All Black play that was admired worldwide.

Yet, even the All Blacks look ordinary when they lose the initiative. When this happens they lack purpose and do not have the same co-ordination. This was borne out in the World Cup in the game against France in 1999, where there was no purpose or pattern to their play. In the previous season they had lost to South Africa after having a significant lead of 17 points. They became defensive by kicking away possession for field position and gave the initiative to the Springboks, who played themselves back into the game and won. In three Bledisloe Cup matches against Australia, with time up on the clock, they lost because they didn't have enough self-belief. Having the initiative and taking the game to the opposition is about confidence. It is built on a range of attitudes, beliefs and values that give a team the motivation to take the game to the opposition rather than being defensive.

The initiative is gained in a range of ways on the field. It is first and foremost gained by taking the match to the opposition. This is a matter of getting the opposition to hesitate and look at what you are initiating. It can happen in a card game like five hundred. You can get the initiative by dominating the bidding. If you are more adventurous and take chances, the other pair in the game start to feel defensive and fail to act on their hand with the same confidence. They tend to be cautious and only go seven hearts when they could have gone eight, or they fail to force you up – to try to make you over-bid and go down.

In rugby, a team can gain the initiative even before the game begins by the way it prepares for the match. How a team goes about its build-up will help to create attitudes that they take into the match. For this reason it is important to have the team well prepared, disciplined and organised. Often it is possible to tell how well teams will do just by observing their behaviour before they go onto the field. Something can be sensed which tells you which team has the confidence to out-perform the other.

Gaining the initiative

The initiative is gained on the field in a variety of ways. The first is through having possession. Then there is variation. By varying play, you force the opposition to hesitate and watch what your team is going to do before reacting. This makes their defence reactive and they fall into the role of following rather than initiating play. I first noticed this tactic when playing table tennis. My friends were better than I was, but if I kept varying my play it would keep them off balance. The variation helped keep me in the game. Once you have the opposition looking for what you are going to do next you have started to gain the initiative. Early on in a rugby game, moves and variations may not come off because the opposition defence is up on your team, but winning is a matter of continuing to play your game in order to dictate play. This way the initiative begins to build. It is the attitude that goes with this pattern of play that has the impact. Players focus on playing their game and imposing their pattern. They believe they are in control and they are making things happen. This builds confidence. The opposition does not faze them. Players are focused on what they can do. This creates a positive mentality, which permeates the team and can be felt by the opposition.

Having a defined team pattern helps players to focus on how to play the game. The more a team can drag the opposition into matching their pattern the better. Of course, the pattern needs to suit the talent and abilities of players in the team. It may be based on some traditional model that has been established over a period, like All Black rugby. One year the team I helped coach had dominance in the lineout and an exceptionally good first five-eighths who could put the ball out at the other end of the field with a wipers kick. We developed a pattern of play that mounted attacks close to the line. Another year it was based on back play and we scored forty percent of our tries from our own half. Generally, variation of a strong pattern of play is an important part of the mix in gaining the initiative. Random kicking gives the initiative away.

Speed is another factor in gaining the initiative. It is disconcerting if you have ever experienced a change of pace when running in a road race. You get into a rhythm and it is disjointing to have to pick up the speed. This is particularly so when it is initiated by the other runner. Such tactics are common in a bike race. There are often breaks from the bunch and jockeying for position in the sprints at the different stages. Transferring this to rugby means picking up the tempo of the game at particular stages. This can be just before half-time when teams are a little susceptible in their defence. Giving a seven to eight-minute burst then can be advantageous and there is the break to recover. Straight after half-time the team trailing on the score board often come out fired up and there is a need to turn that around if you have the lead. A crucial time seems to be twenty minutes into the second half. That seems to be a particular psychological point in the game. It is when players start to feel the physical pressure of sixty minutes of rugby and are more vulnerable. It is a matter of catching them at this weak point and undermining their confidence. It is like the change in pace during a race. It is disconcerting and subconsciously players can feel they are losing the game. Boxers do this. They have to pace themselves through twelve rounds but recognise at certain points the psychological vulnerability of their opponent and lift the tempo to put him away. In a rugby game the captain needs to recognise these opportunities and exhort the team to a supreme effort. This should happen two or thee times in the course of the match.

Initiative and confidence

The main feature in gaining the initiative is the attitudes of the players as a team. It is their confidence and determination that makes it happen and it is reflected in their will to win and their team spirit. A good coach should emphasise statements such as, 'We want the initiative,' or, 'Seize the initiative.' Often in a game the initiative swings between teams. At lower levels, it is possible to hold the initiative for extended periods, but it is more difficult to achieve at top levels. Having the initiative is clearly demonstrated when a team is a couple of points behind with a few minutes to go, and yet is being strongly offensive. They finally score and then the game reverses with the other team doing all the attacking. It's not that the first team loses so much energy that they can then only defend. The change is psychological. It is essential to keep uppermost in players' minds the need to gain and keep the initiative. The old motto, 'The best form of defence is attack,' refers as much to keeping a psychological advantage as to a physical one.

Initiative and defence

Building the initiative is a state of mind that creates the psychological edge. It can be demonstrated by asking, 'When we have the ball, what should we do?' The answer is 'Attack.' Again, 'When they have the ball, what should we do?' Most players will be tempted to say 'Defend'. That's not what gaining the initiative is about. When they have the ball, we should attack! That is a totally different attitude from what most teams take when the opposition has possession. You are attacking, ball or no ball. When the opposition senses this attitude you have the initiative. Creating an offensive defence has been the linchpin for the Canterbury Crusaders in winning Super Twelve titles. Similarly, General Patton mastered mobile warfare as an effective tactic. He never went to ground when under fire, as that was the area where the enemy had zeroed their guns. Instead, he drove through and attacked. This tactic kept his adversary off-guard and in constant disarray. They never had time to regroup. The initiative was very much on his side.

Initiative and try-scoring mentality

Another important focus, besides the concept of gaining the initiative, is identifying the objective of the game. The old Otago coach, Vic Cavanagh, highlighted that the basics of the game were the three P's of rugby – Position, Possession and Pace. I have also taken three P's as the objective of the game. However, the three P's I have identified are different from Cavanagh's. The first P stands for 'points.' What do you think the second and third P's stand for? The answers given to this question vary, from pressure and physical skills to peak performance. For me the second P is 'points,' and guess what the third P stands for – yes, you have it, 'points!' The focus of the game is points, points and more points! Bob Dwyer sums it up when he says 'Rugby is a game that deserves to be played positively, by which I mean every team should be willing to risk defeat in the pursuit of victory. If your primary aim is to avoid defeat by avoiding risk, you are better off not playing rugby at all.'[3]

Most players are 'line shy' – they don't commit themselves to scoring tries. While some players will go for the line, most look for support and someone else to score the actual try. An analysis of try scorers in a team usually shows that they are only a few select players. Some are in key positions, such as on the wing, where they get more opportunity to finish off movements to score, and then there are a few others who score regardless of their position. Usually there are only three or four who consistently score tries during the season. With emphasis on the three P's it is likely that nearly all the members in the team will score tries. Training should develop the attitude in players to hunt and score tries.

When I hear 'Pressure – pressure – pressure' as advice from the sideline I know the team is not really focused on the objective of the game. One of the best cries is 'Points (team name), points'. And then after they have scored call for more points! It can also be very effective when your team is in its own half or even inside their twenty-two and supporters are calling for more points, even though they are supposed to be defending. Another call is 'Go, go (team name).' It is positive. Too often negative comments are made from the sideline. By barracking from the sideline it is possible to encourage a team to gain the initiative.

One of my best personal experiences of this try-scoring mentality was when I was coaching Bernie Fraser at secondary school. He later became an All Black, and 'Bernie's Corner' on the left-hand touch was named after him at Athletic Park where he got many tries. In a first XV college game against Auckland Grammar, the ball had been kicked through and was bouncing in the corner of our in-goal area. Bernie had managed to out-sprint the opposition to get back a few metres ahead. One supporter beside me grabbed my arm and started yelling, 'This could be dangerous! This could be dangerous!' Would you have any idea what he meant? You may have guessed. Bernie scored under their posts! There was no cover defence so he was able to run across his in-goal area, out by the posts and then had half the width of the field to manoeuvre around tacklers. With his superior speed, he was able to score without a hand being laid on him. In that situation, the first thing that came into his head was 'Points, points, more points.' I told this story to a Wellington taxi driver when he was taking me to Bernie's pub. All of a sudden he went quiet and then said, 'He did that to us when I was playing for Wainuiomata!'

An earlier lesson of the value of points, points and more points was learned from an incident after a club game when I was playing with a young Mark (Twig) Sawyers. Twig later became an All Black. In this particular game he took off from our twenty-two and side-stepped through nearly the whole opposition team – he only had the fullback to beat and our winger was outside him with an overlap. Instead of passing he tried to go around the fullback and was dumped. The crowd instantly reacted and he knew he had got it wrong. At the after-match function Mick Bremner came up to him (keep in mind Mick was a very formidable All Black from the old school), and asked if he saw the winger outside him? Twig said, 'Yeah.' Mick then asked if he heard the crowd boo? 'Yeah.' And then Mick surprised me by saying with a big grin, 'Isn't it great to commit yourself to the line?' Mick understood the importance of thinking points. While Twig got it wrong, he wouldn't have got as far as he did if he hadn't backed himself. The number of tries he made for himself and others in the team more than compensated for the few times things didn't work out.

The importance of thinking try-scoring came to my attention when the locks in our team decided to have a pre-season bet about who could score the most tries. The loser would have to take the winner and his girlfriend to dinner. In the previous season, neither had scored a try. As it turned out, one scored four tries and the other scored five. The last try was controversial. As one lock barged his way up-field and was held up short of the line, he turned to feed and found to his horror that it was his locking partner coming through. There was a momentary hesitation before he fed the ball – and that was only when his mate was dead parallel to him and there was no one else. On the way back to the halfway line they had a roaring debate about whether that one should be counted.

In earlier days the line was called the goal line. This was because rugby originated from soccer. There were no points for forcing the ball over the line. All it did was give the scoring team the opportunity to kick for goal, and that was how they got points. It is only the goal line for the kicker. At practice I line the team up and make sure that they understand that for them it is the 'try line.' Once this sinks in, players will push themselves to the breakdown in order to get the opportunity to score points. Often the tries are unspectacular but, as one friend said to me, his hockey coach had taught him that 'all goals are good goals,' no matter how unspectacular they are. He learned to run straight at the goal to score goals, regardless of the whacks he got from hockey sticks.

'All tries are good tries!' Often those unspectacular tries are the ones that make the difference. Usually in an easier game the backs cut through and pile up the points. When the game is tighter they get chopped-down short of the line and it is up to the forwards to finish off the movement. It is only when they have a try-scoring mentality that they seek out the opportunities to make tries happen. I also remind players about the definition of when a try is scored. Most think it is when downward pressure is placed on the ball over the line. To me it is when the referee awards it!

Building up this try-scoring mentality is an essential part of success. We don't go out to beat the opposition, but to out-score them. Our whole game is based on scoring points. This is quite different from the focus of most teams. For years the catch cry has been 'No mistake rugby,' which only highlights the points I made earlier. The focus is on not making mistakes. The best way to make no mistakes is not to try being adventurous! Yet tries go to the doers, those who are adventurous. In nearly every game players find that they will have an opportunity to score if they are in the right place at the right time. It is a matter of pushing oneself to chase those opportunities.

'No mistake rugby' is not the purpose of the game. Sure, you don't want to make mistakes at crucial phases in the game. In fact, you only need two minutes of no mistake rugby in a game. It takes less than twenty seconds to score a try from anywhere in the field. That means that if you can string together four or five tries in a game in those two minutes you will have over 20 points, not counting conversions and penalties. This is the whole thrust of

'Points, points and more points'. It is twenty-second bursts of outstanding rugby adding up to two minutes. It is a matter of putting together try-scoring opportunities.

Some supporters take exception to this approach about try scoring, saying that it breeds selfishness. This has never been my experience. I have found that for every try we missed because we should have passed the ball we scored nine through determination to make the line. The emphasis is on scoring for the team. Building commitment to the team is an integral part of the approach I advocate in coaching, and scoring tries fits within this context. To counter-balance the egotism that can be displayed when a try is scored, I insist that the team immediately jog back to the halfway line. This stops them doing high-fives and other self-congratulatory gestures. I don't mind if there is a spontaneous expression of joy for a great try, but it shouldn't be egotistical as seen in American football and as is creeping into our game. Some expression happens at times when the players are naturally overjoyed with the try. The understanding is, however, that they jog back to the halfway line and watch the conversion from there. It looks very professional and stops inappropriate behaviours that are detrimental to the spirit of sportsmanship.

Once, when I was a guest coach to a senior team in the Bay of Plenty, we had a flanker who didn't quite believe in the points, points and more points philosophy. At practice, he held back a little in attempting to score the tries. On the Saturday, the game opened up very quickly and the ball was bouncing short of the opposition's try line. He was there on the spot, but anxiety caused him to fumble the ball and miss the opportunity to score. He learned the lesson and at practice focused on gathering the ball and crossing that try line to score. He became one of the top try scorers in the Bay that season, after scoring only one try the previous year. He came to realise that pushing himself when the breaks were on, making sure he was in support and going in for the ball at the breakdown rather than waiting for something to happen made a difference. He could also identify other players, like Hika Reid, who were also try-hungry. When you have fifteen players who have the killer instinct to go for the try line, points are bound to come. Most players go out onto the field not thinking about scoring. They should almost feel uncomfortable with the tension inside themselves to want to score a try.

The points, points and more points philosophy leads to a more expansive game. Players get greater satisfaction and excitement when the team is scoring points. The Super Twelve competition's bonus point for scoring four tries encourages this approach. Even if you are behind on the scoreboard, the team is still trying to close the gap and get four tries for the bonus point. This is a great approach and captures the spirit of rugby. Rugby teams should focus on out-scoring the opposition. To the credit of rugby, the administration has experimented with bonus points to encourage this to happen.

Summary

This chapter pulls together the overall concepts that are important in gaining a psychological edge. Essentially, it is understanding the attitudes, beliefs and values that create excellence. When achievement values are present, the team will perform to high standards. Gaining the initiative allows a team to dictate play and gain ascendancy. This gives both a psychological and tactical advantage. The focus of play is on points, points and more points.

---

1. Graham Henry, *The X Factor*
2. John Wooden with Jack Tobin, *They Call Me Coach*
3. Bob Dwyer, *The Winning Way*

Chapter 2

ACHIEVEMENT MOTIVATION

Creating excellence is what sports coaching is all about. Excellence is what distinguishes outstanding individuals and teams from the others. But what are the keys to creating excellence? We can all describe an end state when asked about excellence. It can be identified in the turnaround the Warriors have made after being at the bottom of the Australian rugby league table for five years. Auckland and Canterbury rugby teams have had sustained periods of high performance and so have produced a large number of All Blacks. The Brumbies are a good example. They were originally made up of leftovers from New South Wales and Queensland, yet they performed better than the other two state sides in their first year and went on to be in two finals and win the Super Twelve competition. The question is: What were the driving forces that got them there?

Achievement values

In the previous chapter I mentioned that many coaches have difficulty describing their success even though they have been able to create excellence in their teams. The distinguishing characteristic of these outstanding groups is high achievement values. Therefore, a starting point in building your understanding of outstanding performance is to know what achievement values are and how to build these attitudes. Many effective coaches are only partly aware of the factors that make them stand out. If they are unable to fully define or accurately describe what the factors behind achievement motivation are, how can they develop them in others? In appreciating the underlying thinking of high achievers, you will be able to foster this motivation in players and the team. This book provides an x-ray of the anatomy of excellence and forms a basis for helping coaches help players excel. This is what Alexander the Great believed was of the utmost importance: 'I assure you I had rather excel others in the knowledge of what is excellent, than to extend my power and domination.' The pursuit of excellence is firstly about creating high achievement values.

The difference in thinking between high achievers and others is often subtle and not always easily discerned. There is only one or two strokes difference between Tiger Woods winning a masters tournament and the other players. But he is able to constantly produce the concentration and performance that make the difference. That is what excellence at the top is all about. The thinking behind excellence will become more obvious when one has a fuller appreciation of the values of achievement. This is an aspect of psychology that I have spent over twenty years studying and measuring, in conjunction with some of the best researchers in the United States. We found that high needs for achievement characterised most successful individuals and groups in commerce, sport and society in general.

Professor David McClelland first studied achievement motivation at Harvard University. He wanted to figure out why some people were more motivated to improve themselves and perform better than others. What was the driving force within these people that led them to devote their energy to improving their skills? He wanted to tap into the motives these people possessed, and find out what generated their sense of excitement in facing challenge and using their skills to compete. He started by examining the way in which high achievers thought. He wanted to know whether they thought differently from others and if this difference could be described and measured. He found that high achievers did think differently from others and that these differences could be defined. More importantly, he found that such attitudes could be developed in those who did not have particularly high achievement thinking. This is of fundamental importance in the approach I advocate in coaching. Achievement motivation is the desire to do things better, to improve performance and to feel positive about challenges. This spirit is captured better in sport than in most other activities.

There are several factors that are important in developing an achievement-oriented team. Such groups enjoy testing their abilities by constantly trying to do things better. They are challenged by tasks that require skill, and take personal responsibility for their performance. They try to find more effective ways to reach their goals. This enjoyment of performing tasks and continuing to learn from their effort leads to an even greater insight into how they can improve and attain higher levels of performance.

Since Professor McClelland's early work, a wide range of research has been done on the beliefs, attitudes and values that distinguish those high in achievement from others.

Some key themes associated with achievement are outlined below:

A willingness and desire to set goals

One outcome of an achievement-orientated way of thinking is a preoccupation with self-set goals. So when an individual or team starts focusing on setting and attaining goals they are tapping into achievement-orientated values and behaviour. For high achievers this is a natural thought process. Almost unconsciously they think in terms of what they want to achieve. When they set goals, those goals tend to be high but achievable. In fact, high achievers have an in-built radar that guides them to assess accurately what is possible and to set goals that stretch their abilities but are still attainable.

Setting goals is part of any sporting endeavour. Often it is neglected in rugby. It is not that you just set one overall goal. The idea is to identify concrete objectives that your team has a 70 to 75 percent chance of achieving. Don't make them too low, as they must provide a challenge. Don't make them too high. Once goals move beyond a reasonable chance of success they quickly lose significance. Players know when the odds are stacked against them and they will quickly lose motivation. Research on high achievers shows that they generally set their goals at a moderate level of difficulty – one at which they have a reasonable chance of obtaining. Others without such motivation are more inclined to set their goals too high or too low. High achievers also keep upping the ante on their goals as they attain success. They continually seek improvement from their current position.

Golf is a good example of a game that encourages goal setting. People get really hooked on the game even though they may only have mediocre handicaps. They get a sense of progress from mastering the skills. Being on a 12 handicap and getting it down to a single figure is a great challenge even if it isn't going to win titles. In fact, it is likely to make them less competitive in the club champs. That doesn't matter so much; they think more about competing against their own standards and get excited about improving their handicaps. There is something intrinsic about this sense of accomplishment. I like watching the three-hour marathoners finish. The sense of satisfaction they show at getting under that time is immense.

Achievers set goals related to skill, not chance. This is often not the case with non-achievers. In a simulated sports coaching scenario I have developed, many show they do not have a proper appreciation of goal setting. The exercise usually generates heated debate. Participants have to come to a consensus in their group about what is a realistic goal. The scenario outlines goals that range from ninety percent down to only fifteen percent attainable. There is even another choice of not setting a goal at all. Some go for a minimal goal that doesn't stretch their abilities. Many do not set a goal at all, but prefer to take each game as it comes. Others go for a goal that is far too high. A smaller number make a choice which estimates that there is a fifty to seventy percent chance of success. This is in the range selected by high achievers. Once the goal goes below fifty percent, motivation starts to decline rapidly. At that point, players feel their effort will not make that much difference. When the odds are roughly fifty percent, achievement-oriented players can be greatly motivated. It is then that they feel most strongly that their effort can make the difference, though they don't set all their goals at that level because it would be too demanding. The outcome of this exercise shows that most people do not know how to realistically assess their abilities and the level of risk in goal setting.

Goal attainment creates a sense of satisfaction for high achievers. They derive enjoyment from being involved in a task and achieving an outcome. The satisfaction comes from inside them. It is not done out of a sense of obligation or responsibility but by having pride in doing things well. Being goal directed gives a sense of purpose. This is healthy, not only in sport but also in life. Such people gain more satisfaction, are more productive and usually experience far less stress than most people because they know what they are about. Things are not done to impress others but for their own satisfaction, which they get from involvement in their sport. This is seen in professional sports when athletes say it is not the money that drives them but the love of the sport.

Mountaineering is a great example of what I am talking about. It is a personal challenge. Few others will know if a person climbed a mountain. That doesn't matter. It is the sense of challenge and pushing beyond the ordinary that is the driving motive for the climber. When coaches are able to develop that spirit in a rugby team a powerful group dynamic begins to form. Setting goals at the individual level and within the team taps into this drive. It needs to be done jointly so players are part of the process and accept the goals. It is not just a matter of setting goals – this can be over emphasised and not enough attention may be paid to what needs to be done to accomplish those goals. Goals need to be broken down into specific objectives so progress can be monitored.

Achievement is about doing things well

Achievement is about doing things well, and to improve something is a natural incentive for high achievers. They appear to be at their best when they are involved in something that is not easy and requires them to work hard and think through their actions in order to get results. The intrinsic satisfaction of improving something drives them to look for opportunities where they can have influence. There is an underlying belief that there is a better way of doing things and they actively explore alternatives in order to make improvements. Seeking to do something better often implies doing it differently from how it has been done in the past. It may involve finding a new or more effective way of achieving the goal. The very fact that achievement-orientated people are always challenging themselves over tasks means they continue to learn from their efforts, which leads to greater insights into how they can improve and attain greater levels of performance. Their skills continually improve. This is what underlies striving for excellence.

Attraction towards success

High achievers are attracted towards success rather than avoidance of failure. Yet two thirds of the general population are trying to avoid failure. Watching some games, it becomes evident that most players are trying to avoid doing anything wrong. This is the hangover we have about 'no mistakes.' A player can think it has been a good first half because he has not done anything wrong – he hasn't touched the ball at all in the first half – whereas the achiever wants to get the ball to show what he can do. Anxiety about failure is the biggest single inhibitor of producing achievement in sport. Too often the message is 'Don't screw up.' This discourages moderate risk taking and destroys achievement values. Achievers are optimistic about what they can achieve. They have usually had an encouraging and supportive background that has helped to build their optimism. Too much negativity and criticism can destroy this confidence.

Consistency of effort

Achievers give their best, not just as a one-off effort but consistently. They are able to maintain high standards of performance. They are more persistent when working at a task if they think the goal is achievable. They have high levels of aspiration and are not put off by failure. They are able to imagine success. The visualising techniques that players sometimes use are designed to induce this type of thinking. It can be artificial if done in isolation without a value system that supports achievement, but for high achievers this is part of their natural thinking style.

A belief in cause-and-effect thinking

There is a strong belief in cause and effect thinking in high achievers. Once again, two thirds of the population don't think in these terms. Sometimes listening to talk-back radio you would think that no one does. Cause-and-effect thinking helps high achievers to develop strategies and break tasks down into manageable parts, analyse what is necessary, practise these components and master the skills. This style of thinking is the opposite of believing in fate, luck or chance. Cause-and-effect thinking leads to good problem solving.

Many think that it is the 'bounce of the ball' that decides the outcome of a game. Others believe that lucky grounds or historic records are proof of the likely outcome. The sports reports are full of this type of analysis before a game. Those who practise cause-and effect-thinking believe things happen for a reason. They feel a sense of personal control about influencing outcomes. They don't make excusses when things go wrong but try to figure out the cause of the problem. They know that it is not always possible to identify all the causal factors relating to a specific event, but nevertheless exert a good deal of effort in trying to think it out and get a better result. This cause-and-effect thinking builds a greater appreciation of the strategies and skills that are needed to play the game.

A belief that individual effort makes a difference

Achievers believe they can make a difference, so they always do their part no matter how insignificant it may seem. They want to do well and are willing to work hard to achieve results. They have high aspirations and a lot of initiative. Generally they get things right. They are incisive thinkers and are highly motivated. They bring enterprise and energy to whatever they are doing and try hard to do well. They will develop skills to be very effective at their chosen goal. They retain a primary belief that their effort counts. They try to figure things out and to discern the cause-and-effect relationships in what they are trying to make happen. This analytical ability causes them to be more effective. They are characterised by a strong ability to make things better. Such an approach has a 'why not?' attitude. Most people don't feel that their effort makes a difference. Achievers will act independently to make things better. It is an unconscious pattern of thinking that is different from that held by many people.

Desire for feedback

A key to continuous improvement is constant feedback on performance. The term feedback originally came from rocket engineering. A rocket sent into space sends signals back about its progress and corrections are made if it is off target. High achievers respect honest and direct communication. They do not feel defensive about mistakes and want to work out how to improve. Feedback is a measure of performance. Achievement-orientated individuals constantly seek to know how they are doing. There is a sense of enthusiasm in tackling challenges and aspiring to higher levels of performance. Their feelings of satisfaction come from accomplishment. They find it frustrating not knowing how they are doing. They use feedback to monitor progress and inspire improvement.

Confusion about achievement values

Along with achievement, encouragement needs to be given to players to develop them as individuals. Achievement concentrates on task mastery and self-set goals. There is a need to balance this with being player oriented. The encouraging style, in combination with achievement, is the most effective way of coaching. This means giving support to players and recognising the need for teamwork. This balances player and task considerations in order to attain excellence. If achievement is the primary style without a concern for players, tasks will be accomplished but the coach may not be quite as effective as he could be in moulding the team together.

Achievement is about judging oneself against one's own standards of excellence. While winning is enjoyable, it is not the ultimate criterion by which to evaluate performance. This is in contrast to those who have a competitive view and a need to demonstrate their superiority by winning over others. The paradox is that in competitive situations those with achievement values are better able to produce winning performances. When facing competition, achievers have confidence in their own ability, analyse how they need to perform, focus on the task at hand and have a strong belief that through their own efforts they can succeed by doing their best. They do not feel particularly threatened by rivals. Instead, their motivation is heightened by the sense of competition and belief that they can perform well. This lack of egotism means that achievers can accept and learn from failure, even if they have performed well. Their focus and concentration is superior to those who feel that failure is unacceptable.

Another style of thinking that is in contrast to achievement is the power style. It associates self-worth with the need to dominate and be tougher than others. It is an aggressive attitude to life and the need to be on top. Such players are hard men. Their aggression can be channelled into rugby and they have an uncompromising approach to the game. They can be loyal, dedicated and have a high degree of commitment to the game. They have the warrior code. They are continually on the offensive. Such qualities can be admired on the rugby field.

Perfectionism is also confused with achievement. Rather than work to make things the best they can be, perfectionists need to seek flawless results and can be too hard on themselves. Players who are perfectionists do attain high levels of competence and can excel in sport. They are very demanding on themselves because nothing is ever good enough. They set unrealistic standards, which practically guarantee a sense of failure. They tend to be excessively concerned with mistakes and are somewhat driven to try to attain impossible standards. Rather than learning from mistakes, they become frustrated and stressed. They can perform well but there is an associated cost of anxiety and stress. On the other hand, high achievers experience little stress because of the constructive way they approach learning skills. Their self-esteem is not on the line, unlike the perfectionist who is excessively concerned about avoiding mistakes. These competitive, power and perfectionistic behaviours will be dealt with in more detail in later chapters.

Summary

High achievement values are what distinguish outstanding individuals and teams. It is a way of thinking that is associated with excellence. It results in superior performance. This chapter describes those attitudes, beliefs and values. It also points out the difference between achievement-orientated thinking and competitive, power and perfectionistic styles of thinking. These other styles can be detrimental to performance.

I have taken material for this chapter on achievement motivation and other styles from research my company, Human Synergistics International, has conducted. It is copyright to Dr Robert Cooke and Dr J Clayton Lafferty and used with their permission.

Chapter 3

LEADERSHIP STYLES

Coaches have an intensity and fervour about their role that attracts attention. People want to be associated with someone who provides inspiration and excitement. The media attention and hype that surround games builds up their personalities. One thing is clear from all this: the leadership qualities they project have significant influence on others. The ultimate goal of good leadership can be defined as '. . . the art of mobilising others to want to struggle for shared aspirations.'[1]

Why are particular coaches successful? The criterion most commonly used to evaluate a coach's performance is the extent to which their team wins. Results do count. However, there are many different influences that should be taken into account in evaluating coaching performance. This could be the increasing skill of the players, their commitment to the team, how the team rises to challenges and whether they perform up to expectations. These criteria would augur well for developing the team's future performance. Often it takes time for a coach to build a winning combination. It is, however, the coach's leadership that has the most significant influence on the performance of the team and its success.

Effective leaders create focus

Leaders are results-oriented individuals and results get attention. They highlight the importance of goals. Goals give direction in terms of what the team wants to accomplish. This encourages movement and by definition a compelling sense of purpose. Leaders create enthusiasm about what can be accomplished. Their sense of purpose coupled with commitment draws players together. Such coaches do not have to coerce players into wanting to join in the effort. They are often so enthusiastic and intent on what they are doing that they hardly notice the magnetic effect they are having.

Leaders communicate in a compelling way. Goals raise expectations. The team has to believe that something good has to happen or it will never eventuate. Setting goals is important, but paying attention to what needs to be done to accomplish those goals is even more important. Too many coaches over-emphasise the goals without the accompanying strategy of how to reach them. It is vital to tell players precisely what you want from them. Sharing this information focuses what they must concentrate on and helps the coach to co-ordinate the team better. Leadership, then, is a process where the coach sets the purpose for the team and then gains the players' complete commitment and dedication to the cause.

Build trust with the team. Coaches who are trusted make themselves known; they are consistent in their behaviour and can deal positively with all the hassles that come with managing and running a team. The only way to get this respect is to earn it. Players have to recognise that the coach's actions are not motivated by his ego, but by a desire to have them do their best. This trust is of the utmost importance. It is behaving in ways that act as a role model and set a standard for others. Personal example is a powerful way to influence the behaviour of those around you.

A positive self-image is a key component of a successful leader. The concept you have of yourself influences how you communicate as a coach. Those who are achievement-orientated give players the opportunity to develop independent thought and action. They like to see them enjoy challenges and the comradeship of the team. The starting point for urging players to improve is to be aware of the values, beliefs and attitudes you hold and how they influence the way you think and behave as a coach. These thoughts and feelings are part of your self-concept and have been built up from past experiences, your environment and other people who have influenced your life. Outstanding coaches know themselves. They know their role as coach can be distorted by unresolved needs or past agendas that cloud their judgement. Socrates' sage advice was to first 'Know thyself.'

The way you think influences the way you set goals, your ability to handle stress and your effectiveness as a leader. Don Shula, the winningest coach in American football history, says, 'In the long run, winning coaching has more to do with the coach's own beliefs.' He has also said, 'It's the coach's – the leader's – beliefs that are most important; they become self-fulfilling.'[2] Recognising your strengths and compensating for your weaknesses is the first step in developing as a coach. Effective coaches are generally psychologically healthy individuals. The media are inclined to portray coaches as being tough and demanding. This can be the impression some coaches project but a closer examination will reveal that most effective coaches are much more supportive of their players than is portrayed publicly and are far more constructive in their behaviour than is popularly recognised.

Constructive leadership is a matter of balance and perspective. A good leader creates a climate that is positive, and reinforces the goals that the team is striving to achieve. These leadership responsibilities can be carried out in a number of different ways. They include a mixture of positive and restrictive strategies. The emphasis is on being positive but it should be kept in mind that coaches also need to deal with problems of discipline and poor performance if they arise.

Effective coaches keep working on improving their skills and developing a positive regard for themselves and their players. Effective coaches are able to recognise some of the flaws in themselves and the way they respond to situations, and make adjustments. Like their players, they set goals and objectives for themselves to improve. It is this capacity to develop and improve that sets outstanding coaches apart from the others. It is not that they start out with all the necessary skills but they learn from their experiences. From these experiences they are able to reflect and adjust the way you think and behave so they become more constructive.

Positive self-belief will transfer to players. This is why people are attracted to those who display such healthy attitudes and behaviours. Under such a coach, players are more willing to accept direction, know they can count on the coach for support and feel encouraged. Underlying this is a whole range of assumptions about motivating players. They are based on a belief that players are willing put forth extraordinary effort to achieve team goals if an environment is created which supports and reinforces achievement-oriented values. Coaches with positive self-regard rarely need to rely on coercion to get players to perform. They are able to tap into players' intrinsic motivation. While such coaches do criticise their players when needed, they first build unconditional support and belief in their abilities. They then set about helping the players refine and improve their techniques.

Players need high self-esteem if they are to have confidence in facing the pressures that sport presents. Realisation of their own potential is closely associated with high achievement values and their self-esteem. When players feel positive about themselves they are much more likely to attain higher levels of performance. They set their expectations higher and are more willing to take risks to achieve their goals. This is why building players' self-esteem is an essential ingredient in coaching. To do this the coach first needs to respect his players. Such regard is built from the coach's positive view of himself and the world of sport. This helps to create enthusiasm, spontaneity and imagination in players so they have a sense of excitement about the game. Such a positive regard for players does not blind the coach to the less desirable qualities they sometimes display, but focuses on the strengths of each player and encourages positive reinforcement. Many talented players have failed to reach the heights they are capable of because they haven't had the confidence.

Attraction towards success is a fundamental value in the high achiever. If members of a team keep thinking about avoiding failure, they are more likely to be hesitant and uncertain about their abilities. The impressive thing about effective leaders is that they focus on success. Failure doesn't worry them. It is not that they have been protected from failure in the past. Instead there was encouragement and support for doing well. Such experiences build attitudes that overcome the fear of failure. It is like climbing a cliff and looking up, rather than looking down and losing confidence. When you attempt a new skill there is every likelihood that at first you won't succeed. Failure is not a sign of lack of progress. Each time you make a mistake something is learned and you figure out how to improve. It is not that achievers necessarily enthuse about failure but realise that it is a springboard for improvement. High achievers learn from their mistakes and are not discouraged. They are willing to go into situations knowing that they may get it wrong, but also knowing experience is necessary to gain the knowledge and skills to achieve higher levels of performance.

Most people in the general population don't really believe in success. They have low achievement-oriented values. They feel threatened when in a situation where they need to make things happen. The fear of failure holds them back. They have learned to treat failure as a strike against their self-esteem. They become overly hard on themselves. When they make a mistake it is difficult for them to forgive themselves and move on. This results in anxiety and the feeling that they should avoid situations that carry the risk of personal defeat. No doubt in their past they have felt condemnation because of failure; it has affected their morale and the view they have of themselves. It is better to play it safe or cover up mistakes than to deal with them directly.

Teams that deal with mistakes constructively perform better.

How a coach deals with mistakes and corrects them will influence the climate created in the team towards playing an expansive game. In sport, learning and extending skills continuously takes place, so it is obvious that mistakes will occur. An attitude where the word 'failure' carries negative connotations means mistakes will automatically produce discouragement. In a survey we have used worldwide, one question that told us more about the organisation's culture than any other was: how does your company deal with mistakes? When there was a climate of blame, there was avoidance of responsibility and little got done.

Achievers are noted for their persistence in the face of failure. If they believe that they are capable of making the grade they will keep trying. This is why they need encouragement to persist in refining their techniques and skills. It is important to recognise the improvement they have made. All too often players only hear when they make mistakes. It is not necessary to say, 'You dropped the ball.' They know they dropped the ball. Clamping down on mistakes may help to eliminate them but players will be inhibited from trying anything adventurous. Remember that the game goes to the doers and the doers are the ones who make mistakes. One American coach used the prayer of Pope John, 'Be aware of what is going on around you. Overlook the things that don't matter. Work towards getting better every day.' That is a prayer that every coach could use.

Achievement-oriented coaches inspire their players to improve. These coaches have a positive regard for players and optimism about what they can achieve. You need to display this in your approach to coaching. It is not just a matter of being liked, but of doing the right thing. If a coach tries too hard to be popular, it can be self defeating. Achievement-oriented coaches appeal to their players' desire to strive, to stretch their ability, to improve continuously and to go beyond their present level of performance. Such qualities, when present in players, are a predictor of success. The emphasis is on improvement. This becomes the guideline for creating excellence.

Achievement values, and encouraging style, combine to form the most effective coaching style. Members in high achievement groups are task oriented. In a team they can enjoy the expertise each individual brings to the game. They work well together because they appreciate each other's skills. Teams like the Chicago Bulls, under Phil Jackson, are able to dominate their field when they achieve this. Jackson was also able to develop in players a positive regard for other members in the team. Building players into the team is a key function of the coach. The Notre Dame football coach, Lou Holtz, says, 'Never underestimate the positive effects that love and compassion can have on a team. Creating a caring atmosphere is not a complex task. Simply follow the golden rule to treat others as you want to be treated.'[3] When a coach concerns himself with the welfare of players, he engenders loyalty and respect.

Players look for competence and integrity in a coach. Care must be taken to demonstrate competence. It is not about creating the impression that as coach you know everything. That is being a perfectionist. Effective coaches don't assume such knowledge. They have the ability to work with others and develop ideas. They are willing to listen and experiment with new ways of doing things that lead to innovation and greater effectiveness. They demonstrate their competence and integrity in the way they share their ideas and facilitate discussion.

Counter-productive techniques

Adopting artificial techniques to motivate players is counter-productive. It is contrary to the true spirit of coaching. There must be deeply held beliefs supporting coaching techniques. Players see through insincerity. Using inappropriate techniques in an attempt to manipulate players doesn't bring out the best in them. Such techniques could include: appealing to their competitive instincts, vengeance for a loss, hatred of the opposition, or fear of failure. Threatening players '. . . to be committed to the team or they will get dropped' is acting like the wolf in sheep's clothing. It is advocating a positive value but in a coercive way. Similarly, lip service can be given to concepts such as teamwork when the input of others is not really valued. This creates cynicism about the motives of the coach. Effective coaching is not just a matter of applying some motivational technique, but of expressing deeper beliefs that are consistent with building confidence and teamwork. It has to be a holistic approach, representing a range of attitudes, beliefs and values that support achievement and other intrinsic motives in players.

Too much emphasis can be placed on the rules and routines that a team must follow. While some conformity is necessary in any team, too much insistence on rules discourages personal responsibility. It is more effective to build up attitudes that target commonly held goals and values. This will lessen the need for rules. For instance, I have never had compulsory practices but players have always been keen to be there. It is almost a punishment if they aren't allowed to practice. Having built a strong commitment to the team, players feel they would be letting down their team mates if they weren't there. Creating expectations like this is more important than rules. Any rules should be rational and jointly agreed to by the coach and the team.

Coaches need to realise that there is more than one way to deal with a situation. Two coaches in the same situation can behave quite differently. One coach in a situation may feel threatened, while the other feels exhilarated. The difference in response is in the way they think and interpret the situation. High achievers look for co-operation to achieve the desired outcome, whereas coaches with more aggressive/defensive styles of thinking feel the need to exert control and authority. Take the example of players coming late for practice. This could lead to the coach laying down the law and rebuking offenders. It could lead to sanctions such as fines or dropping the player for the next game. Rod Macqueen used an alternative approach when faced with this situation. At his first practice session as coach of the Waratahs, he found players were joining training 20 minutes late. He didn't say anything. Instead, after practice he told the players that in future they would train hard for 90 minutes and training started after the last player arrived. The next practice was a little late but after that they always started on time. There hadn't been a confrontation between the coach and the players. Macqueen knew it was important for the team to take responsibility for themselves rather than him laying down the law. The power-style coach would have confronted the players who were late and created some resentment.

Another common mistake is to be detached from players by constantly being critical, pointing out the faults and dealing with mistakes. The coach becomes exasperated with mistakes and his relationship with players deteriorates. While some social distance may be advisable, a coach needs to be able to relate to players. Coaching isn't a role where the emphasis has to be on being critical and negative. When things aren't going well it is possible to fall into this mode of thinking. Players find it difficult to be motivated under a critical coach. Such coaches tend to have a watchdog approach. Constant criticism keeps players on their toes but fails to bring the best out of them. Video playback and other statistical information on things like incorrect lineout throws can create this negative emphasis. For most players it doesn't work, and results in frustration and a lower level of performance. Pointing out what is done well and encouraging more of the same creates excellence. The paradox of coaching is that players learn more from their successes than they do from their failures. Missing a tackle doesn't teach a player how to tackle.

Shaping the leadership of the captain

The captain of a team needs to be aligned with the coach's philosophy and management style. This means consulting and involving the captain in all the issues around managing the players and developing the team. In this way the captain is part of the decision-making process and is committed to the outcome the coach wants to achieve. This is one of the important bonds in the formation of the team. The captain needs to know what the players think and should inform the coach of issues that may need to addressed. There is also a need for the captain to show leadership and set a positive example. Ultimately the coach needs to be responsible for appointing the captain. There can be input from others. At top levels, much more responsibility is put on the captain. This includes dealing with the media, managing relationships during tours and being able to call the tactics during the game, particularly when the game plan needs to be changed. Giving a person such responsibility in their mid-twenties will be a big learning curve. The coach needs to mentor the captain to help him or her gain an appreciation of the role and how they can work together.

Often the leadership on the field is spread among senior players or key positions in the team, rather than being the sole responsibility of the captain. The first five is in a pivotal position and regardless of seniority has a decisive influence on the strategies and tempo of the game. Others also contribute – Sean Fitzpatrick was ably assisted by players like Zinzan Brooke and Grant Fox. Jeff Wilson also contributed. The captain is a rallying point on the field. His inspiration and actions set an example and are a prerequisite for high performance from the team. The key players do have to read the flow of the game and adjust tactics as the game evolves. The captain needs to keep the team's focus on gaining and keeping the initiative and countering the opposition's strategies. Captaincy is about leadership on and off the field and making adjustments as the game evolves. The team must learn to work with the captain on decision-making, strategy and communication. Members also need to appreciate the team dynamics that influence this process.

Alan Border, the Australian cricket captain, was an outstanding example of a good leader. He took over the captaincy when Kim Hughes broke down in front of the cameras after losing another test. At that stage a joke was going around Australia asking 'What was the difference between the Milford Track and the Australian cricket team?' The answer was that not everyone had walked over the Milford Track. Border had to lead a losing Australian team. In all his interviews he kept reinforcing achievement values. He kept identifying where the team was making progress and how it could improve. He kept his own game up and would not be put down by the media when the team lost. His example turned the team around and, with the same players, they went on to become world champions. Australian cricket has never looked back from that time and has gone on to excel in the international arena.

Coaching and the encouraging style

Coaches with the encouraging style motivate and help players gain enjoyment from the sport. They are supportive and help them to grow and develop. Such coaches encourage and treat everyone with respect They are aware of players' needs and provide positive feedback. They are actively supportive, put a good deal of effort into training, and share their ideas with players rather than imposing them. They show trust and confidence in their players. They share decisions with those affected by them. Their focus is on continually helping players improve their performance through encouragement.

Often coaches do not want to get too involved in the difficulties and conflicts that arise between individuals in a team. It is necessary to deal with any problems that may be affecting the team. Failure to do so can lead to unresolved conflicts affecting the team's performance. The coach needs to be able to counsel the team in such situations. This is part of the encouraging style. When there is a lack of cohesion in the team the coach should do everything he can to discover the cause. This can mean calling a team meeting and not letting anyone leave until the problem has been uncovered. Most players prefer a fair and negotiated settlement to a state of unresolved conflict. Once a player was asked: If you were in trouble, who would you call, a priest, a doctor or a lawyer? The answer was his coach, Vince Lombardi, because he was all three. Avoiding dealing with difficulties in a team lowers morale. It is not that you want to spend your time looking backwards, but resolving problems and moving on is the key to getting the best performance from a team. The emphasis is on helping them to grow and develop.

Coaching and the competitive style

Competitive coaches emphasise winning as the goal and aren't afraid to go after what they want. Everything is evaluated in win/lose terms and this creates a competitive spirit in team members.

The emphasis is on the excitement and satisfaction of being a winner. While winning is not a dirty word, studies show that those who come out ahead in competitive situations focus on performance excellence. The process of doing well, which is achievement oriented, is quite different from an emphasis on winning and being admired.

Often competitive thinking can be confused with achievement values. While competitive thinking is largely encouraged as a measure of success, it is not an effective way to predict achievement in sport. As has already been mentioned, those who come out ahead in competitive situations focus on performance excellence, the process of doing well, rather than on winning. Bob Dwyer, the Australian coach, used to explain the difference when he repeatedly said, 'I don't want people who want to win, I want people who want to prepare to win.'[4] For the competitive player, winning provides a sense of satisfaction and self worth. By beating others, they fulfil their need to be recognised and praised. Failure to them is unacceptable. This strong competitive drive comes from the need for attention. Being victorious equates with feeling superior over others. They do not seek excellence but only want to win. Contrary to what many think, most Olympic champions and successful sportsmen do not think this way. Competitive thinking is not what drives them.

At one stage a series of television advertisments was run showing overseas swimmers and other athletes looking into the camera and saying in a very intense way, 'I am going to beat you!' as a way of getting people's involvement in the upcoming games. The general public reacted very critically to these advertisements and they were pulled. The ads did highlight, however, that even those at the top level of sports administration had no clear idea about the values they were supposed to be engendering.

The drive for competitiveness is reinforced in terms of rewards, social pressure and cultural values. Many, including the media, place great emphasis on winning in sport. This results in some players seeing everything as a contest where they have to beat others in order to receive recognition and have feelings of self-worth. This makes losing particularly difficult as it results in a loss of self-esteem. Such players can't accept this and can rationalise defeat or go into denial. The win/lose emphasis distorts their perspective. Underlying this behaviour is self-blame and anxiety about losing. They need to continually demonstrate their superiority to boost their egos, which in turn gives them a sense of satisfaction and security. Losing is humiliating to them. They are constantly building themselves up and want to be seen and noticed by being better than others.

This pre-occupation with winning and being admired causes competitive people to overestimate their abilities. They generally like to be the centre of attention and can be boastful. They get upset over losing because they try so hard to be successful. If they win they feel good, but if they lose they feel worthless and defensive, and such defensiveness means they don't learn to improve. Their belief is that 'winning is everything.' This attitude means their self-esteem is dependent on their opponent's performance and not on what they can achieve. Losing doesn't mean that you didn't play well and should dump on yourself. The pursuit of excellence is where the real rewards lie, not in beating someone else. Achievers don't let their self-worth get tangled up with the result.

I once had a player sitting beside me before a game and I asked him what he wanted to achieve. The answer flashed back, 'Win.' I asked him how he was going to do that. 'Don't know,' came the reply. That guy didn't have many clues about performing. The best comment on the difference between achievement and competitiveness I have come across was when golfer Arnold Palmer was asked why he was losing to Jack Nicholas. His answer was, 'I go out to beat Jack and Jack goes out to play good golf!'

Competitive attitudes tend to hype people up, and that is why they are promoted by the media. The pre-game hype focuses on competitiveness and beating the opposition. Results are always evaluated in win/lose terms. There is confusion between achievement and competitive thinking. Dealing with the media is often a contrast in styles. The media see the game in competitive terms, while captains and coaches are usually achievement oriented. The media always go through a patter of having the losing side feel disappointed. For some reason they think everyone must feel depressed in the dressing room if they have lost. If you win you receive approval. This emphasis reinforces competitive values and the need for approval.

Graham Mourie was interviewed after a game against Scotland once and commented that with fifteen minutes to go Scotland were still in the game, then the All Blacks scored a try, a penalty and then another try near full time to put the game beyond doubt. The television interviewer then turned to the camera and said, 'Scotland, forty points scored against them, are they good enough to be an international side?' They then interviewed the 'losing captain' – not the 'Scottish captain.' Yet with fifteen minutes to go, Scotland were still in the game! To the media, winning is everything and you rub the loser's nose in the dirt.

Competitive coaches place an emphasis on winning and getting the support of the media and fans. While high achievers enjoy such support it is not their primary motivation. The competitive mentality is attention-seeking and egotistical. Competitive coaches place an emphasis on winning and appeal to the competitive spirit in players. It does get a response and heightens motivation. However, this emphasis has side effects that do not enhance team performance. One of my sons was in a schoolboy team where the coach would tell them the selectors were coming and if they wanted to make the primary school reps they would have to play well. Each kid was out to get selection and played selfishly. Yet the coach thought that was building the right mentality before a game. He was building the competitive motive. That coach also thought he was building teamwork by telling the boys to pass the ball, but when the big second five got the ball he would yell, 'Run Rangi' to the detriment of teamwork.

Competitive coaches pit players against each other as a way of motivating them. This technique can develop intense and destructive rivalry within a team. In a Chicago Bulls practice, Phil Jackson once ran a drill that pitted the guards against the centres. When Michael Jordan went one-on-one against Bill Cartwright, Bill had such a fierce look in his eyes that a silence fell over the court. Cartwright bumped Michael as he went up and sent him flying horizontally through the air. It was a chilling experience for

Jordan, even though Bill cushioned his fall. Needless to say, Jackson didn't use that drill again.

While a certain level of competitiveness can be stimulating, too much leads to the team becoming fragmented. The win/lose orientation causes members to treat others in the team as opponents rather than allies. They end up competing against each other, even though they are expected to work together as a team. This was demonstrated in New Zealand's early challenges for the America's Cup. There was an A and a B team, and an intense rivalry developed between them. While this produced intense motivation it was also disruptive. The bowmen on the two yachts didn't speak to each other. This approach did get us through to the Louis Vuitton final. In the challenge, when the Cup was won under Peter Blake, a different philosophy was in place. Team members were rotated on the boat and everyone identified with the team effort. While merit did have its place in selection, some having more races in the cup, there was not the same rivalry as in the previous challenges. Yet many successful coaches erroneously attribute their accomplishments to being competitive, when in reality they have been achievement oriented. Contrary to what many believe, most successful coaches and players do not think in competitive terms.

Competitive attitudes can easily be inculcated in youngsters. Attention and recognition is given to kids when they win. There is disappointment when they lose. Soon they get the message that parents approve when they win. There was once a KFC advertisement on television showing little 'Johnny' coming off the football field with dad giving him attention as they walked over to the car where mum was waiting. It was all smiles, and dad announced, 'We won.' After that the music plays and it is all happy faces and KFC. Maybe it would have been baked beans for losing. 'Johnny' soon realises that winning is how he gets approval and his parents can't understand why he gets temperamental and upset when he is losing. They don't realise that they have created in him a belief that if he loses his parents do not hold him in the same regard. One kid I coached was paid if he scored a try. This could have made him selfish. Instead he took quite a sensible approach by telling the others to pass him the ball to let him score and the money would go into team funds. Avis Rental Cars sums up the right attitude with their slogan, 'We're second, but we try harder' to compete against Hertz.

At one stage I was involved with a school team where the coach had achieved little success. They had never been in contention for a championship. The coach's approach was friendly and supportive but lacked the push for excellence. After introducing my philosophy and achievement approach, a dramatic turnaround took place. The team won two championships before I finished assisting the coach. A few years later I rejoined when another son was going through the school. It was disappointing to see the change that had taken place in the intervening period. The coaching philosophy that had been grounded in achievement values was now a mixture of power, competition and achievement. The coach had a lack of insight into the attitudes and values that had earlier been engendered. Other influences had come into the coaching approach. An All Black selector had assisted when his son was in the team and winning had become too important. Practices were more aggressive and the approach to matches was competitive. The emphasis was on making the semi-finals and the championship.

One incident, which typified the situation, was at the end of the year when the team was withdrawn from the semi-final play-off because the key lineout jumper was sick and the prospect of losing was too much. This reflects the intensive beliefs about winning and losing of the competitive coach. Achievement means going out and facing the odds, even if they are running against you. The main criterion of performance for the team is to play to the best of its ability. If the boys had done that then they would have had the self-satisfaction of knowing they had done their best and it would have been a great way to finish the season. Instead, it finished at practice when they were told they had been withdrawn. It was one of the most disappointing moments in my association with sport.

This is not just a phenomenon of junior teams. The All Blacks suffer rejection if they don't win. The New Zealand Rugby Union can be harsh on a losing team and the media play it up. It is seen as an incentive for them to do better next time. This is a misinterpretation of the values associated with achievement. The sports jocks are the ones who buy into this way of thinking. When the All Blacks lost the final in the World Cup in South Africa they were welcomed back with an enthusiastic ticket tape parade up Queen Street in Auckland. It was almost to their disbelief. They had played well and lost the final in extra time after many were battling food poisoning. The general public recognised their tremendous effort. However, the loss to France in another World Cup was met with shock, horror and criticism. It was not the loss that exasperated the New Zealand public, but the fact that the All Blacks played without spirit. They then repeated this disappointing effort with a poor performance against South Africa in the play-off for third. It was obvious the attitudes weren't right in the team.

Another aspect of competitiveness is when players start to think they are on a pedestal and believe what everyone says or writes about them. This is egotistical and associated with competitive thinking. What drives achievement-oriented players is not the adulation but their love of the game. What tears a team apart is when players believe the team can't do without them and they want to be the centre of attention. They try to prove that they really are as important as the fans and media think. Such people are full of themselves and are generally the ones who ignite power struggles. The day Phil Jackson took over the Chicago Bulls he vowed to create an environment based on the principles of selflessness and compassion. This is in total contrast to the attitudes associated with competitiveness.

Competitive and egotistical behaviour can also be seen when the media start to glamorise players. The attention inflates their ego and invariably leads to a fall in their performance. Carlos Spencer is an example of too much attention being given to him as a glamour pinup boy. He started to draw attention to himself with his blonded hair rather than concentrating on making his mark as a rugby player. When he finally wanted to excel at the game again, he regained All Black selection and played some of his best football. It can be hard for a young player to focus on his game when he gets that much attention. Maturity helped him to overcome this distraction.

Matthew Ridge is a player I would identify as having highly competitive values. His former coach, Graham Lowe, described him as having an arrogance that he simply didn't like. He believed that Bob Fulton, who succeeded him as coach of Manly, made Ridge too macho and he developed a superiority complex. While it may have helped his football, it didn't help his personality. It brought out a selfish streak and made him a bit of a bully. Malcolm Boyle, who bought out the Warriors with Lowe, described Ridge as a captain who never motivated the younger players. 'His competitive attitude upset and unsettled some of the team. Most of them were Polynesian kids not used to getting a burst. He would climb into them and these kids even had difficulty making eye contact.'[5] A transformation in performance took place when Daniel Anderson took control with a different coaching philosophy.

Besides the egotistical aspect of competitive thinking, it creates a belief in luck, which diminishes real skill on the football field. This is opposed to cause-and-effect thinking and a belief that one's own effort will make the difference. Such things as fancy moves, or trick passes that aren't thought out, are typical of this type of thinking. When such moves come off, the media are full of admiration and give a great deal of attention to them. They are repeated in television clips and everyone goes, 'Wow, aren't they great!' This is precisely the media attention they seek. Sure, it pays to toss the ball over your shoulder right on the touch line on attack and hope someone in the team catches it so it will result in a try. It is another thing to do that on defence or other unlikely situations. There needs to be better judgement when to take such risks. The high achiever takes calculated risks, while the competitive thinker is reckless. They do not think out their decisions. If the impossible comes off they are boastful. The Warriors have fallen into this trap by being big-headed over a great win, and then losing to a bottom team the next week because they thought it would just happen for them. It can also be seen in some of the antics players get up to after scoring a try. They need to be able to get the balance right. I believe in chancing your arm when you have the initiative and are going forward. In test matches, players have to be more calculating because mistakes are severely punished.

Wayne Bennett, from the Brisbane Broncos, said, 'There's nothing wrong with ego so long as it's healthy, one which promotes confidence but still allows its owner to be part of a team, one which promotes leadership even without the captaincy, yet realises the owner is not indispensable.' He believed: 'One guy full of himself, and the team's in trouble. Two or three and the team has no chance.'[6] In contrast to this is a team member who is honest, direct, and can be relied on by other team members. The problem for competitive and egotistical players is when they have a slump in form and are copping criticism they don't know how to handle it and have difficulty overcoming the setback.

While winning is widely accepted as the way of measuring success, the competitive style is not an effective predictor of performance in sport. The song 'We Are the Champions – no time for losers' is pathetic. It is the antithesis of achievement attitudes and displays abysmal values about sport. Yet many adopt the view that a highly competitive style is effective and confuse this with the pursuit of excellence. The distinction is important, since the quality of performance is generally higher when it arises through a drive to achieve rather than a focus on winning. Competitive players give a priority to beating others. Losing, to them, means diminished self-esteem. In fact, they can become angry and dejected when they lose. Such a mentality breeds a dread of losing and this threat can adversely affect their performance.

Coaching and the power style

In contrast to achievement values is the power style, which keeps a tight reign on players. If you have learned to be tough minded and aggressive it will be portrayed in your coaching style. Players dare not think for themselves and the team lacks the ability to take the initiative and lift their performance. The power style may work in isolated cases, but usually it creates resentment and frustration in players. There was a time when that type of approach could get results, but the modern player will not readily respond to that sort of control. Often it is exerting control through fear. It could be a player's fear of making a mistake, fear of embarrassment, fear of losing the game, being verbally abused or dropped from the team. If part of the coach's belief is the need to dominate and control others, this type of behaviour will emerge. When it causes conflict and a break-down in team performance, the coach just gets more stubborn and bloody-minded. This has a negative effect on the players and they become more guarded.

Initially the power style can get a lot done, but it is less effective than many think, because coercion and punishment are poor motivators. Such coaches enforce standards and exert their authority in order to maintain control. They are dominating and like to feel in charge at all times. They are task oriented and lack confidence in players. They feel the need to be forceful and coercive to get results. They can be intimidating and quick to anger. They can judge team members harshly and things get done at the expense of team members' confidence. This stifles initiative and the opportunity for players to develop. Initially this behaviour can look like strong leadership, but continuously directing and giving orders is a poor substitute for letting players think for themselves.

Some coaches think they are at their best when they are being powerful and aggressive in their behaviour. There may be times when a coach does need to take a stern and decisive approach. There is no doubt that a shake-up can have a salutary effect if it is warranted. There is a difference here between a coach who is constructive and a coach who is power-oriented. The first will focus on performance and show respect for the players. In a game the passions flow, but anger without compassion degenerates into abuse and tears the fabric of the team. There are times when it may be necessary to lay down the law, but it needs to be done intelligently. As much as possible, a positive emotional environment has to govern the team. Always keep in mind that most players thrive on positive reinforcement. They can only take a certain amount of criticism, and they will become demoralised if they are criticised too personally.

Power-oriented players accept an autocratic style of leadership.

They expect the coach to exert authority and will respond well to demands placed on them. In fact, a style of coaching which allows more input from players can be anathema to them. They like tighter control and direction from the coach and will accept abuse and criticism as motivational. This helps to fire up their anger. It means they tend to subscribe to increasingly aggressive and driving play. Such players can be disruptive in a team if they are not getting their own way. This applies particularly at senior levels when personalities are more dominant or when they have a leadership role in the team. Their negativity toward things they don't like can be destructive. It leads to criticism, blaming others and not accepting the responsibility to work co-operatively. Channelled properly in sport, these attitudes can be turned around so the player makes a more worthwhile contribution to the team. In the end, achievement motivation triumphs over power as the effort is better focused and just as determinedly pursued.

While some team members accept the authority of the power-oriented coach and exhibit similar aggressive behaviours, most resent the way they are being treated. They tend to defy the coach's authority indirectly through sub-optimum performance. The result is a team that lacks initiative, drive and eventually the ability to perform. Yet, in spite of this power style, such coaches and captains still get appointed and this style is thought effective. It is a fallacy that players respond well to that type of leadership. Rugby does attract those who have aggressive personalities. This behaviour is confused with the assertiveness associated with achievement-oriented coaches. Such coaches have a confidence that comes from the positive regard they have for themselves and others, as well as a constructive focus on tasks. This attitude has quite a different impact on players. In professional rugby, coaching is becoming more sophisticated; it is evident that power-oriented coaches have not got results and a number have been phased out of coaching contracts. Frank Oliver, a hard man of rugby who unsuccessfully coached Wellington and Auckland, was typical of this style. The Warriors suffered this sort of coaching under Mark Graham, with the same consequences.

Being angry and criticising players may get an instant response and a jump up in performance. This can justify the actions of the coach. The problem is that with each succeeding outburst there is a declining effect as players become conditioned to such treatment. Repeated abuse means the coach ups the ante in order to get the same effect, and this leads to cynicism and demoralisation of the players. As one American football coach was reported as saying, 'Every coach carries a six-gun into a season. It's got six bullets and a coach can only hit his team between the eyes those six times. He has to be real careful about when he does it, or even if he does it.' My advice is to keep one in the chamber in case it has not been a successful season. You may have to use it on yourself!

It is a proven myth that the power style produces top performance. Psychological data collected by my company on over 35,000 managers and leaders in New Zealand and Australia shows clear statistical evidence that power behaviour is negatively correlated to effectiveness. Unfortunately this style still tends to get promoted. On the surface such executives seem to have their act together but over time their lack of ability to lead and motivate others has a detrimental effect on the business. They get results but at a cost, and that cost leads to a breakdown in performance.

The same happens in the military. A study of military commanders in a book called *The Psychology of Military Incompetence* showed that the great military defeats were the result of generals who were so power-oriented that they blundered into battle believing in their own dogmatic views and not taking cognisance of the real situation. This was typical of the First World War generals. In contrast, the successful campaigns were characterised by high achievers. Such generals as Douglas McArthur were innovative in their tactics and constantly kept the enemy off balance. McArthur was the first to appreciate that an army could be supplied by air. The DC3 became the workhorse. This meant that he could keep the enemy off guard by attacking behind their positions hundreds of miles along the coast. In contrast, the tank was never properly used in the First World War even though it had been invented in 1912, before the outbreak of hostilities. Innovation is one of the hallmarks of achievement thinking. The power style of thinking hinders innovation.

Coaching and the perfectionistic style

Just as there is confusion over power and competitive values versus achievement, so there is between achievement and perfectionism. A perfectionist coach is after flawless results and is not satisfied with anything less. This thinking is a characteristic of a number of successful sportsmen and women.

Players who are perfectionists tend to see themselves as highly effective, and seek to master all aspects of the game. There is, however, a difference between striving for perfection (achievement) and trying to be perfect (perfectionism). While many successful players have a degree of perfectionism, an excessive concern with this style of thinking leads to being overly detailed and losing sight of what really needs to be accomplished. Besides being hard on themselves, perfectionists are also prone to criticising others rather than being constructive. There is the tendency for them to remain aloof and detached from others because they are too task focused. They are highly judgmental and not even the best efforts are good enough.

John McEnroe typifies perfectionistic behaviour. As a tennis star, he was known for his excessive anger and frustration on court. He couldn't tolerate a linesman who made a miscall. In his autobiography, he mentions that when his agent, Gary Swain, first started working for him he told him that he needed sawdust before every match because '. . . I used to keep [it] in the pocket of my tennis shorts . . . to absorb the perspiration on my hand.' When Gary turned up with the wrong kind of sawdust John screamed at him, 'You call that sawdust? [It's too fine!] It looks like rat poison. Can't you get anything right?' Similarly, when he missed a shot, he once told spectators, 'I'm disgusting. You shouldn't watch. Everyone leave!' He says that a good deal of it was directed at himself. He said he grew up very competitive and perfectionistic and still considers himself to be. He thinks it's about not being satisfied. Ultimately, he thought it harked back to not enjoying competitive tennis that much – being too afraid to lose.[7] While he attained high levels of performance, it was at considerable personal cost and his temperamental behaviour caused him to lose matches he should have won. It is hard being in the cauldron of intense competition.

While it can be an effective way of thinking to master finely tuned skills, demonstrated by Grant Fox's goal kicking, perfectionism is counter productive in a coach. The coach may feel driven because nothing is ever good enough, but there is too much anxiety about something going wrong – a fear mistakes will let the side down. Mistakes happen in sport. A coach can't be driven by the need to avoid all mistakes by trying to make things perfect. Such an approach results in being too focused on minor errors and trying to ensure everything is technically right. The role of the coach is to create an environment where players take responsibility for getting things right. Although we think of perfectionism as a way of obtaining excellent results, it is really self-defeating. In the end it causes coaches to become frustrated and burned out because of the excessive demands they put on themselves.

Adjusting coaching styles

If power, competitive and perfectionistic styles (aggressive defensive styles) are not excessive, and are balanced with the constructive styles of achievement and encouragement, they lead to an effective style of coaching. Challenging ideas, asking probing questions and working hard to obtain quality results are all part of being a coach. This helps to get to the heart of any problems. Similarly, a certain degree of power and competitive behaviour is necessary. The coach needs to be self-assertive, expect loyalty, be forceful when required and have a 'be a winner' philosophy. It is a matter of balance and choosing behaviours that are appropriate to the situation. High achievement-encouraging coaches are a combination of authoritarian and democrat combined. They seek information, clarify, set standards, encourage calculated risk-taking and seek action. They seem to have perspective on situations and act appropriately.

However if coaches are too much into the aggressive defensive styles they will have a negative impact on the team. With the power style, the tendency is to be driven to be in charge at all times. Such coaches are forceful and dominate others. They intimidate and coerce players. The competitive style needs to win at all costs. They have always to be right and constantly think of life as a contest. Their manipulative behaviour is designed to build their own ego. The perfectionist coach is driven to prove himself and rarely feels a true sense of accomplishment. These styles need to be modified.

The relationship between a coach and players is often fraught with tension because the coach is constantly evaluating each player's performance. A team typically finds the negative and oppositional behaviour of coaches difficult to deal with if it becomes excessive. Coaches can become too critical and assume a negative attitude towards almost everything, focusing intently on problems rather than solutions. Instead of having a constructive approach to clarify or refine something, they typically point out the flaws. A coach of one of my sons would stand behind the posts during a game and rant at them about all the things that were going wrong. This style limits a coach's capacity to be creative. They need to learn to focus on the possibilities and see things in a positive light.

Attention to detail is important, particularly as players move to higher levels. At the top level, success usually accompanies attention to the finer details of the game. This can mean planning practice sessions so they are run efficiently. It means analysing in depth the skills that are to be taught and the patterns of play that need to be developed. It is about striving for excellence. It is about meritorious performance and surpassing previous standards. It is the gradual result of always wanting to do better. It is a matter of concentrating on moderate and sustainable improvement. This is different from perfectionism, which continually demands perfect performance.

Changing thinking and behaviour

It is not the purpose of this book to go into the intricacies of behaviour modification. It is about disciplining yourself and consistently monitoring the way you think and act. Your attitude and actions should be compared with achievement and encouraging styles to see if you are following similar patterns of thought and behaviour. In planning change, you should seek support from a trusted friend or personal coach. The outcome is greater self-understanding and an improved ability to coach. It will give you an appreciation of your potential strengths and areas of development that will culminate in greater satisfaction and success.

An example of changing one's thinking is how John Konrads, an Australian Olympic swimmer, learned to alter his competitiveness. He outlined his experience to me. At the Rome Olympics, John won two individual medals, a bronze and a gold. He claims the bronze resulted from an over focus on competitive thinking, the gold from achievement motivation. In the 400-metre freestyle, where he came third, his focus was too much on the daunting figure of triple gold medallist and arch-rival Murray Rose. He remembers losing focus on himself by worrying too much about what Rose was going to do. 'As soon as I started thinking those thoughts I had blown my chances. Obviously, I got on the blocks and tried to persuade myself that I could win but the negative thoughts overtook me and the focus was on the competition, the occasion and the rivalry between us.' This thinking produced small but fatal flaws in his swimming; for example, lifting his head at each turn looking for his competitor. Not only did he lose to Rose but another swimmer in a wider lane got the silver. After Konrad came third in the 400, Don Talbot, his coach, immediately wiped the experience by focusing John on the 1500 and an achievable goal. John remembers very vividly his feelings before the race, 'Butterflies in the stomach mixed with serenity,' resulting in winning the gold.

When John came across my company's work on achievement and competitiveness he identified with what he now calls his 'competitive disease.' He says it is a life-time challenge; 'It's a challenge that is winnable through self knowledge.' John believes the first step to overcoming competitiveness is awareness. Once you are aware, you can move through to acceptance and action. 'The best action is to back off and focus on yourself and don't worry about it. The easiest way to avoid competitive learning is to shift from the importance of the occasion to completing the immediate task. Don't think in terms of winning and losing.'

Another tip John gives for moving from competitive thinking to achievement-based thinking is to focus on internal standards – personal best (PB). That is something swimmers can achieve. If they train hard, peak at the right time and prepare well, they produce their best. John recalls the old Boy Scout chant: DYB DYB DYB 'Do Your Best.' He also talks about setting realistic achievable goals, not unrealistic goals. 'For example, don't focus on the Olympic gold medal when you should be focused on winning the local club championships.' When playing squash, his other sporting passion, he constantly reminds himself to focus on the ball not the man – 'I stare at the ball to avoid focusing on my competitor.' John applies achievement thinking in all his business dealings. He was managing director of the Australian branch of an international company and he now runs his own business.

It is a matter of understanding what you are now and what caused you to be that way. There is a need to recognise the consequences of such behaviour and how it affects you. Then it is a matter of deciding what aspects of your thinking and behaviour you need to change. This means developing a specific strategy to make changes. The outline of John Konrad's experience is a fine example of change and personal growth. Coaches like Rod Macqueen have talked about how they learned to adjust their behaviour and overcome some power and perfectionistic qualities they possessed. Psychologically healthy people aren't perfect people, but they learn from life's experiences and adjust. This idea is perhaps summed up in the words of psychologist William James when he said: 'The greatest discovery of my generation is that human beings, by changing the inner attitudes of their minds, can change the outer aspects of their lives.'

Achievement and encouraging styles (constructive styles)

Being able to inculcate achievement values in players and the team culture is the most important contribution a coach can make. This is achieved by the way the coach encourages and develops players so they constantly strive to improve, think for themselves and become committed to the overall performance of the team. The encouraging style, when used by parents, brings out achievement values in children. Children should not be overly protected from failure but given ample opportunity to try new and different things. They are not punished for doing poorly but praised for doing well. It is the same for rugby players. Under such coaching they quickly learn to improve their level of performance.

The values of achievement and encouragement highlight the ability to make things better. It is a healthy and positive outlook. Coaches who follow these styles expect the best. It is a natural, down-to-earth style with a certain zest for the game. How they think guides their lives and they are motivated by their own values. They have a desire to work actively towards a sense of collaboration. They are perceived as realistic judges of situations. The styles have relative freedom from feelings of guilt and worry. Such coaches have an optimistic view of life and a high level of self-confidence. They exude a sense of excitement and generally have a high level of accomplishment. Peter Blake had such qualities. They are the best-of-the-best qualities in a leader and a coach.

Summary

In this chapter I have reviewed leadership qualities and how the coach goes about creating values associated with excellence. These are expressed through the attitudes, beliefs and values of the coach and the coach's leadership style. Paramount are achievement and encouraging styles. Such coaches are insightful in diagnosing problems and help players strive to obtain quality results. They expect loyalty, can act forcefully and are interested in gaining influence. This is based on merit and what is good for the team, which is in contrast to the power, perfectionistic and competitive styles that have a counter-productive impact when such behaviours are excessive. Too often a player's potential is under utilised because of the power and competitive behaviour of the coach.

This chapter has called on the work of Bennis and Nanus – 'Leaders.' The description of the competitive, power and perfectionistic styles are copyright to Dr Robert Cooke and Dr J. Clayton Lafferty of Human Synergystics International and used with their permission.

---

1. Kouzes and Posner, *The Leadership Challenge*
2. Don Shula and Ken Blanchard, *Everyone's A Coach*
3. Lou Holtz, *Winning Every Day*
4. Bob Dwyer, *The Winning Way*
5. *Sunday Star Times* (24 November 2002)
6. Wayne Bennett, *Don't Die With The Music In You*
7. John McEnroe, *Serious*

Chapter 4

LEADERSHIP STRATEGIES

There is not one type or model of a leader. Early research tried to identify leadership styles as being dependent on the characteristics of the groups they lead and the tasks to be accomplished. It was suggested that leaders should take an authoritarian approach if the team had low readiness to perform the task in hand. This means using a highly directive and non-supportive leadership style. While this may work in the short term, it won't build trust with players. It is likely to be dysfunctional over the long run. Players learn that they are expected to do as they are told rather than use initiative. They are presented with a role model that emphasises close supervision and one-way communication, to the extent that players accept these expectations. The acceptance of this role model simply reinforces the need for direction. Such attitudes are revealed when top players are told they are professionals and they should motivate themselves. The coach has abdicated one of his prime responsibilities and cops out on leadership.

Another popular idea of leadership is that leaders must be charismatic – that they possess some special gift. At best this view distorts our appreciation of leaders. At worst it can lead to hero worship. Charisma without the skills and knowledge required to coach is ineffective. This is why some outstanding players fail as coaches. Zinzan Brooke is an example. He had difficulty training and motivating an English side. Part of the reason is that he did not serve an apprenticeship. While he had leadership ability, he didn't understand the important strategies coaches use to motivate and develop players. Graham Mourie's great leadership ability and personal qualities didn't quite translate into coaching success.

A good mate, Dr Rob Cooke, who runs a centre for applied research in Chicago, has led recent research on leadership and has developed an underlying theory on the strategies that leaders use to motivate people. I have already mentioned strategies such as being a role model. Rob's analysis of leadership identifies a number of other strategies. Within each strategy there are prescriptive and restrictive strategies.

> **Prescriptive strategies** are those which guide or direct the activities and behaviours of players toward goals, opportunities and methods. **Restrictive strategies** are those which constrain or prohibit certain types of behaviour that interfere with the attainment of goals.[1]

Effective leaders use both prescriptive and restrictive strategies. Prescriptive leadership provides players with a direction in which to channel their efforts. It reinforces and encourages how things should be done. Restrictive strategies can work towards the same ends but through a different route. In contrast to the prescriptive approach, the restrictive strategies tend to oppose and discourage undesirable ways of performing. According to Rob, most leaders, including those who might implicitly prefer prescriptive over restrictive strategies, tend to use both. Effective coaches call on restrictive strategies to a lesser degree.

Envisioning

One of the fundamental strategies of effective leaders is to envision how things should be and communicate this vision. This gives a sense of direction. It includes expressing strong opinions about what the coach likes and doesn't like and behaviours that are inappropriate. The vision includes the style of play and the way the team is expected to perform. It identifies standards of performance, expectations about training and the mission of the team. Included is a strong philosophy about the 'way things should be done around here.' It can outline how performance will be evaluated and what is expected of players. Selection and training policies can be outlined. The restrictive side of envisioning is being clear about what you don't like, viewing certain behaviours as inappropriate or expressing strong opinions against certain ways of playing the game. Overall leadership requires the capacity to relate a compelling picture of what needs to be achieved and communicating how to get there. Communication is inseparable from leadership. The vision needs to inspire commitment and be continuously reiterated. It also needs to be reinforced not only in words but also in action.

Monitoring

Another strategy identified by Rob that effective leaders employed was monitoring. This includes monitoring performance, noticing what is happening and showing support when improvements are achieved. Noticing when things are done exceptionally well is one of the most effective ways of developing excellence (achievement values). It is focusing on what is done right. The opposite is restrictive practices, which is managing by exception. This means concentrating on any mistakes and what is done wrong. While it is necessary to pick up on some mistakes, most can be disregarded because players know when they have made mistakes and will work on improvement without having to be told. This does not mean disregarding all mistakes, but picking up on particular points that are important or where players aren't aware they haven't got it right. This could include being out of position on defence, not running the right lines on attack, some technical aspect of the skills they are developing or the need to work the team pattern more closely.

Feedback

Providing feedback is an essential strategy for improvement. This can have either a positive (prescriptive) or a negative (restrictive) focus. Both types of feedback are critical to any team as there is a need to correct faults as well as to identify what is being done well. The emphasis needs to be on positive feedback. When negative feedback is consistently being given in the absence of positive recognition it lowers morale and is destructive. The coach can show this by being visibly annoyed when things aren't working, criticising and sending non-verbal cues when players are out of line. Once, when running a senior team at practice, I grunted every time they dropped the ball or something went wrong. Nothing was said except for the grunts. By the end of the practice it was disastrous, everything was going wrong, yet nothing had been said. It was a salient point that I have never forgotten. Letting people know when they have met or exceeded expectations gives them a lift, while constant criticism is demoralising.

Stimulating thinking

Effective leaders have a strategy of continuously looking at things in new and innovative ways. They are willing to challenge the assumptions they make and use input from players and other members of the coaching team to add fresh ideas. Players need to try new things at practice and, if they work, introduce them in a game. For example, Brumbie players questioned why at a 22 drop out they always kicked to the same spot where the opposition had their tallest players. Instead they looked for where shorter players were positioned and drop kicked toward them, giving their own team a better chance of recovering the ball. Within two weeks the shortest player was standing next to the tallest guy. Video analysis had awakened them to the tactic. It means fresh ideas need to be introduced to stay ahead.

Problem solving is an important component in stimulating thinking. It recognises cause-and-effect thinking and goes to the heart of the issue. It means sifting through the options, choosing the best answer and then turning it into action (prescriptive). Players understand the game plan and how their effort will make a difference when they are involved in discussions about the patterns of play that have been set. There is the need to promote creativity and flexibility in solving problems. When coaching is confined to traditional approaches, it promotes conventional play. This does not lead to capturing the initiative during play. Without encouragement the unique talents of individual players are not brought to the fore. Instead the game becomes more controlled off the field by the coach and there is no flexibility to adjust strategies as the game unfolds. Players become so disciplined in the pattern they must play that they stick to the game plan even when it isn't working. They dare not think for themselves and make adjustments (power style).

Influencing

Another leadership strategy is to have a reciprocal relationship with players. This means giving respect to players and being open to their influence. It uses participative methods,ensuring that decisions are understood and accepted. Ironically, coaches who use these reciprocal strategies (prescriptive) enjoy greater influence than those who adopt unilateral strategies (restrictive). Unilateral strategies limit a player's discretion. The coach relies on the authority inherent in his position and vetoes any suggestions. The reciprocal approach relates to the achievement and encouraging styles while unilateral strategies relate to the power style. Coaches need to have an approach that engenders more lateral thought. This is necessary for continual innovation in strategies and tactics.

Mentoring

Effective leaders use the strategy of active mentoring. They explain to players how and why things are done in the team. They create expectations within players to take action and risks consistent with the team approach to the game. This form of mentoring (prescriptive) is central to coaching in that it enables players to more effectively take initiatives consistent with the actions required to achieve the team goals (encouraging style). The restrictive strategy is to let players sink or swim, knowingly let them make mistakes, or expect them to learn the hard way. That creates a fairly negative culture.

Reinforcing

Another leadership strategy is rewarding effort and performance (prescriptive). Conversely, at times it is necessary to deal with poor performance (restrictive). Reward and punishment are two powerful strategies coaches have in being able to shape the culture and performance of their teams. Obviously selection into the team has to be earned and is a reward for those who train hard and perform well. Those who don't meet the standards won't be selected. Players will put in extra effort if they feel they are being recognised and rewarded. Rewards can include raising an individual's visibility, providing more challenging tasks or celebrating their success. The use of rewards has an impact on the achievement orientation of players. The use of punishment breeds competitiveness and perfectionism.

Referring

Referring is a strategy that conveys values through stories. The stories, myths and legends that surround sports teams are powerful ways of bringing to players' attention what the team stands for and the level of performance that is expected (prescriptive). They can be stories of previous games, the traditions that the team should uphold, and lessons from the past. Putting on an All Black jersey is a memorable moment because of what it represents. The same can apply to school or club colours. Stories about previous players and what they achieved serve as inspiration. They can be about sportsmanship and personal commitment as well as what was achieved on the sports field. Negative referents can be about those decisions, actions and behaviours that shouldn't be followed (restrictive). These can be referring to those who didn't fit in to the team or actions taken on the field that were inappropriate. Positive stories tend to create constructive attitudes while negative stories promote defensive attitudes.

Creating a setting

Leaders generally create a setting that facilitates (prescriptive) rather than restrains (restrictive) the involvement of players. When Rod Macqueen took up the coaching assignment with the Brumbies they were a newly formed team. He had player involvement right from the start. When he took over coaching the Australian side he found that the Brumbie players spoke up at team meetings, the New South Wales players made a few suggestions and the Queenslanders said nothing. This showed the contrasting coaching styles the players had been subjected to. Macqueen was able to create a setting that allowed players to grow and develop. He empowered individuals and the team, facilitating a lot of the discussion rather than restraining their contribution.

Constructive and aggressive cultures

The strategies leaders use build constructive or defensive attitudes and values. Prescriptive strategies have a constructive impact on others and restrictive strategies have a defensive impact. Therefore the general approach should involve emphasis on prescriptive strategies. These strategies help to create a positive team culture. These norms and expectations influence behaviour. Teams with constructive cultures encourage members to work to their full potential, resulting in high levels of motivation, satisfaction and teamwork. Members balance expectations to take initiative and think for themselves with a concern for the team. In such an environment, creativity is valued over conformity; co-operation is seen to lead to better results than competition and individual aspirations.

In aggressive cultures, members are expected to appear competent, controlled and superior – shortcomings are viewed as weaknesses. People fall into the trap of believing that in order to be aggressive and competitive on the rugby field, they have to be aggressive and competitive in their approach to training and dealing with each other. They operate on the philosophy that the road to success is through acting tough and promoting internal competition within the team. One current approach to coaching is to develop tough-minded attitudes in players. What does that mean? Is it an appeal to the mentality of power and aggression? Achievement is a way of thinking which has a far greater inner strength. That is the real tough-mindedness.

The Romans were known for their high achievement values. It wasn't that they were always successful in battle, but they never gave in. In their early days, Hannibal, the Carthaginian general, campaigned in Italy for sixteen years and won many victories over them without ever breaking their spirit. Eventually the Romans defeated Hannibal and took over the Carthaginian Empire. Winston Churchill in a short speech to the boys at his old school at Harrow said: 'Never give in – never, never, never.' This is tough-minded achievement thinking, not tough-minded aggressive thinking. He said this in 1941 during desperate days of the Second World War. It is the first lesson I teach any team. When you have a team that won't give in, you have an essential quality for achievement.

Rewi Maniapoto's stand against overwhelming odds at Orakau in 1864, with 320 men and women, when he held out for three days against a force of 2800 British troops, is a case in point. On the third day, when the Maori were short of arms, food and water, the British General called on them to surrender. After consultation among themselves, they hurled back the historic reply, 'E hoa ka whawhai tonu, ake, ake, ake!' (Friend, we will fight on forever, forever, forever). After they repulsed three more attacks, the defenders slipped away in the night. This highlights the spirit of never giving in. I have used that story to inspire teams. It is very powerful when you hear the cry, 'Ake, ake, ake!'

Prescriptive strategies create a positive psychology in the minds of players. Increasing the constructive impact means employing strategies that promote achievement and encouraging styles. This is envisioning, creating a positive setting and stimulating thinking. Such coaches help to mentor players to reach their goals. To decrease the aggressive defensive impact means reducing unilateral decision making, stopping the tendency to continuously provide negative feedback or use punishment as a means of control. It is important to link the strategies leaders use to the impact they have on a team. Understanding these strategies means that you can conscientiously influence and motivate players and create a positive culture in the team.

Danyon Loader exemplified the achievement drive when he won double gold medals at the Olympics in swimming. He said that he had always concentrated on doing his best and to do two personal best times at the Olympics was what it was all about. He said that only thirty percent of athletes at the Olympics achieve their best times and that was what he was determined to do. It seemed almost incidental to him that he got two gold medals. David Kirk, All Black captain, said that winning was not the most important thing to him. 'Winning wasn't the point. Playing the best rugby was the point, and winning was a by-product.'[2] The distinction was real to him. He believed that if all you cared about was winning, if you weren't enjoying the play – if the relief of not losing was the biggest emotional gain – then the best of it was lost.

The restrictive strategies create power and competitive behaviour in team members. The competitive drive is culturally accepted by players and an emphasis on winning is always in the media. Competition can be taught as a way of getting recognition. Coaches can teach competition by using strategies that build on a player's ego or by comparing players to others in order to develop the intensity within the group. The pattern of thinking is to be the centre of attention by proving superiority. It becomes a matter of 'I will win to prove that I am better,' – to get recognition and build self-esteem that relies on the performance of other people. Problems arise because members measure their success against other players and don't learn to set their own standards of excellence. If they win they feel good, but if they lose they are demoralised.

The attempts at the America's Cup under Michael Fay were in one sense successful because the team did get to the Louis Vuitton challenge final on both occasions. The Louis Vuitton is the race-off among the challengers. The approach to team culture was very competitive. Unilateral decisions were made, team members were constrained in the contribution they could make and the leadership was critical and punishing to those who were considered to be out of line. There was an 'A' and a 'B' team and they competed for places on the Cup Boat. They were two distinct groups and competition rather than co-operation marked their relationship. This produced an intense environment and it can be argued that it created a tough-minded attitude that was successful in beating most of the other challengers. However, it didn't create the real excellence needed to win the Cup.

The culture created during the successful attempt under Peter

Blake was shaped in a different way. The leadership strategies that were adopted were much more constructive and achievement oriented. Blake changed the way things were done – for example, in designing the boat. In the past there had been one designer and decisions were unilateral. When it was suggested that there would be a design team rather than one person, the original designer withdrew. In the previous challenge at San Diego, the crew did not know what the boat looked like until they unwrapped it on the wharf. It was a smaller craft designed to be effective in a tacking duel. They then learned to sail it. In the attempt under Sir Peter Blake, which was successful, the design team was responsible to the crew. There was a lot of involvement between designers and crew. The consensus was that boat speed was more important than tacking agility. With the to-and-fro of information, a highly successful design was developed and the team won the Cup with four straight victories. The same policy led to the successful defence of the cup.

There was not an 'A' or a 'B' team in the successful challenge for the Cup. Under the new approach a lot of co-operation took place. Egos didn't dominate. Blake's style was achievement based. While his goal was to win the Cup, he emphasised 'giving it the best shot,' rather than winning. While he wanted to win, he realised that might be something that they couldn't control. Giving their best was something they could do something about. In doing so, they had their best chance of winning. It was expected that everybody would make a difference throughout the campaign. Making the boat go faster was a purpose in itself. They wanted to be one second faster over each three-mile leg. That would give them a six second advantage for the race. The most important gain was the first second, as the lead allowed the front boat to dominate the tactics. In the defence of the cup in New Zealand, the crew rotated on the boat. What epitomised this spirit was when Dean Barker, the understudy skipper, was handed the boat to sail the last race to retain the Cup.

Peter Blake was described as a natural leader. He didn't act arbitrarily. His leadership style was to surround himself with people in whom he had complete faith. He canvassed their opinions constantly, listened to what they said and then helped the group agree on solutions. Internal competition and politics were kept to a minimum. The approach was one of continual adaptation, and once in a while they made a breakthrough in improving the design. Blake would give team talks to inspire the team but he saw that responsibility for leadership lay throughout the organisation. His basic style was described as listen, learn, help and lead. In doing so, he applied strategies of envisioning, role modelling, mentoring, stimulating thinking – and created excellence.[3]

Summary

Leadership strategies either enhance or restrict the performance of others. This chapter shows how the strategies the coach uses can either develop achievement and co-operative values or reinforce aggressive and defensive behaviours. The prescriptive and restrictive strategies employed by the coach have significant impact on the team's performance.

The text on prescriptive and restrictive leadership strategies is adopted with permission of the author, Dr Robert Cooke, from the Human Synergistics Leadership/Impact Feedback Report (Copyright 1997).

---

1. Dr Robert Cooke, *Leadership/Impact Feedback Report*
2. Ken Hodge, *Sports Thoughts*
3. Clive Gilson, Mike Pratt, Kevin Roberts and Ed Weymes, *Peak Performance*

Chapter 5

RUGBY COACHES

New Zealand coaches have revealed little about the strategies they use to motivate players. Their books are usually full of stories about players and games, but not about the psychological dimensions of coaching. It seems our coaches are reluctant to explore the subject. Their books are ghost written by sports journalists who have records of tours and matches, and this information forms the basis of the material for their books. Contrast this with Don Shula, the winningest coach in American football, who wrote a book co-authored by Ken Blanchard, a management guru. Its theme is all about leadership and motivation and not a litany of matches played.

Coaching in New Zealand has become a professional occupation. Our tradition has been amateur sport, with coaches dedicated to run practices on a voluntary basis. There hasn't been an emphasis on developing sophisticated knowledge about motivation. Programmes and tertiary courses are now taught that deal with sport psychology. These tend to place focus on motivating individual athletes to peak performance rather than coaching a team. There is a need for sport psychology to be translated into team coaching. Industrial psychology deals mainly with leadership and management, which is more aligned to team coaching than much of the writings of sports psychologists. Both sport and commerce are achievement oriented. That is why business groups feel an affinity with coaches and sportsmen.

All Black coaches

In New Zealand the modern style of open rugby started under coach Fred Allen with his success with Auckland in defending the Ranfurly Shield. As the All Black coach through the late sixties he established a record that has not been matched, with 14 straight test victories. He was known as 'Fred the Needle,' because of the way he would provoke his players. This entailed stirring them up into an agitated state by using skilfully targeted personal barbs and insults. On one level players knew it was a technique; by the same token, it did get under their skin and got a reaction that aroused their aggression. It is not that he wanted his players to play outside the rules of sportsmanship, but it was his method of psyching the team up. This was the 'psychological' approach of the old school, which had more to do with manipulation than positive psychology.

Allen was on the cusp of a new generation of players. Fred's view of teamwork was when he said 'Jump,' everyone would jump. That was the strategy of an officer leading his men into battle. Fred's attitude grew out of the war years. He saw a change coming one day when he told the team they were going out for recreation and to 'all to get in the bus.' Chris Laidlaw wanted to do something different and after a brief confrontation walked off to do his own thing. This was a new generation of player. Once players would accept being herded about in a group. The break in this type of approach probably came with the end of the Freddie Allen era. He was the last of the Second World War coaches. It was a significant change in the leadership style. Greg McGee's humorous play *Foreskins Lament* portrayed this conflict. It is about an older coach having to come to terms with the values of a new generation.

Regardless of his success, Allen's position as coach was in jeopardy and rather than give the Rugby Union the opportunity to dump him, he packed it in at the height of his coaching career. Being dumped is a reoccurring theme for All Black coaches. As the rugby league coach Graeme Lowe said, 'There are only two types of coaches – those who have been sacked and those about to be sacked!'

Ivan Vodanovich followed Allen. Sports journalist Paul Verdon described him in his book on All Black coaches as the last of the

(Above) 'Attitude is everything. If the attitude was right we would generally play to a high standard and win.' Graham Henry

(Right) 'Rugby is a game which deserves to be played positively, by which I mean that every team should be willing to risk defeat in the pursuit of victory.' Bob Dwyer

(Below) Rituals such as team huddles bring members together into a tightly bound group which symbolises their unity.

(Above) Alex Wyllie's tenure espoused the values of power and achievement. This produced a mixture of motivations in players.

(Below) Laurie Mains astutely combined his practical knowledge of rugby with the dimensions that built achievement thinking.

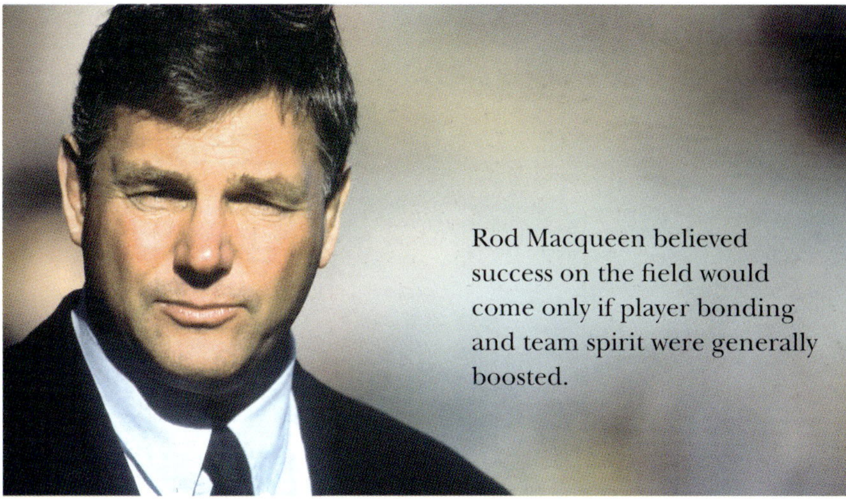

Rod Macqueen believed success on the field would come only if player bonding and team spirit were generally boosted.

(Left) 'You can win and give mediocre effort and you can still lose after giving everything you have. I know which effort I'd be more proud of.' Wayne Bennett

(Below) Power and competitiveness gave John Hart the drive to win, but in the end it lead to over-control and was at the expense of the team continuing to excel.

(Left) While he had leadership ability, Zinzan Brooke didn't serve an apprenticeship to understand the important strategies coaches use. This caused him difficulty in motivating an English team.

(Right) Frank Oliver was a hard man of rugby who's coaching style couldn't get results.

(Below) Graham Mourie's great leadership and personal qualities didn't quite translate into coaching success.

(Above) Bernie Fraser was brought up on the revised 3 P's of rugby. Here he is scoring a try in "Bernie's Corner" at Athletic Park.

(Below) Michael Jones was never penalised for foul play. He didn't hate the opposition. He always had a courteous manner and respect for other players.

Try scorers The revised three P's of rugby are . . .

Points . . .

Points . . .

. . . and more Points!

(Above) The hill draws something out of players that has an extra special dimension. It personifies determination.

(Right) Daniel Anderson turned the Warriors around by helping them to believe in themselves.

The same motivational principles needed in coaching a professional team apply at the amateur level. They are obviously adapted for the level of maturity of the players.

Although pre-adolescents do not tolerate as much work per practice, they seem to recover faster after strenuous exercise.

Lessons on the sports field are far more able to convey and develop achievement values than any subject in the classroom.

'sweat-and-strain, hellfire-belching'[1] coaches. His methods were old-fashioned and it appears he over-trained his side. Verdon reported 'Jazz' Muller as saying he needed more games to get fit for Ivan's training sessions. He did not get the best out of his players. Among the experienced players were some who became disillusioned with his methods. His series losses to the Springboks and Lions led him to make an honest assessment of his effectiveness, and resigning. Bob Duff followed and was probably judged unfairly because of the Keith Murdoch incident, the actions of the so-called Mafia within the All Black ranks, and their loss to the Barbarians.

A breakthrough came with the appointment of John (JJ) Stewart. He had an enlightened coaching style, which involved his players in decision making and responsibility. This produced innovative patterns of play that took into account the law changes that made the back lines stand further apart and allowed for more constructive play. He was able to develop a style of play around the team's strengths and weaknesses. He was skilled at analysing the opposition, developing strategies, communicating his philosophy, and involving everyone in an intelligent approach to the game following prescriptive strategies.

Stewart's style reflected a more liberal approach. This work well with players who were increasingly resistant to slogging it out unquestioningly. They wanted to know the reasons behind their strategies and that their own ideas might be taken into account. One criticism was that he allowed himself to be too influenced by the senior players in choosing a team. Mains, who was a junior member of the team, claimed that cliques developed on the tour and these players dictated the selection. Stewart was, however, a man ahead of his time, and unfortunately this brilliant thinker and coach was held responsible for the failings of the 1976 All Blacks in South Africa and dumped by the Rugby Union upon his return.

Jack Gleeson's All Black coaching career was inextricably linked with the All Black captain of that era, Graham Mourie. The rise of Mourie and Gleeson went hand in glove. Mourie was ahead of his time in his approach to All Black captaincy. Gleeson had a talent for man-management. He was not of the shout-at-them, die-for-your-country school of coaches, a breed that, thankfully, seems to have now died out. His belief was in the importance of getting players to think – 'The whole game is thought; gone is the day of brute strength and ignorance. Rugby is a game of thought. Play the game at pace and be a thinker.'[2] Players responded to Gleeson's approach. Stu Wilson said, 'Jack never waved a big stick. He approached, he encouraged, he coaxed – and above all he made us believe in ourselves.' This once again exemplifies the prescriptive strategies of leadership. Unfortunately, deteriorating health forced him to give up coaching though he remained a national selector until he died a year later.

Eric Watson took over what was a hard act to follow after Gleeson's grand slam All Blacks. Mourie described Watson's style '. . . as honest and simple as the man himself. Rather than take players and develop them into a team, allowing the game to evolve from the individual styles of the group to suit their disparate abilities, Watson moulded the players to his game.' He based his game on the age-old style of low-packing, hard-driving forwards. 'Given the right players, Watson's rugby was unbeatable,' says Mourie. 'But with a team unable to carry out his basics, it faltered. If Watson had a fault, it was that when his side did fail, he tended to exhort greater efforts rather than try something new.'[3] He would not have tried and succeeded like Gleeson did in the second test in Paris. In this game the All Blacks wanted to avoid meeting the French forwards head-on so they gained the initiative by calling short lineouts, moving the ball wide and playing the game at pace. They wore out the big French forwards, gained the initiative and were able to impose their will on the game.

The South African tour of New Zealand in 1981 was a contentious time and divided New Zealand. Peter Burke had to pilot the All Blacks through that series for a test series win. He also had a series win over Australia. Bryce Rope followed. His two-year tenure produced an impressive record of nine wins, two losses and a draw. He was then dumped for Brian Lochore, with a tour of South Africa coming up and the lead into the first World Cup. It was again a contentious time for rugby – legal action scuppered the official tour and Colin Meads ended up leading the controversial

Cavaliers team to South Africa. Lochore could not use the players from that tour and struggled with the Baby Blacks against Australia. The next year he won the World Cup after beating Scotland in the quarterfinal, Wales in the semi-final and France in the final.[4] The success of this All Black team was an outcome of the man-management skills of Lochore, the conditioning methods of Alex Wyllie and the pattern of play used by Auckland, whose players represented a disproportionate number in the team. John Hart revolutionised rugby with the innovations he made to attacking patterns of play.

Alex Wyllie was appointed All Black coach in 1988. He had been a hard and uncompromising player. As coach of Canterbury he had been successful in a new Ranfurly Shield era. He had a reputation as a very aggressive personality and chewed through a number of players before finally producing a team that climbed to those heights. As the All Black coach he inherited 14 Aucklanders in the squad. Wyllie's methods of coaching were in contrast to Hart's. He was seen as a tough but fair coach of the traditional mould. Players like Buck Shelford responded well to his leadership, but it may have hampered his relationship with the Auckland contingent who reacted against the authoritarian approach. There were differences in team culture under Wyllie and Shelford. Politics were to hamper Wyllie's tenure as coach. He felt that he was being undermined, as did the captain, Buck Shelford.

The Wyllie tenure espoused the values of power and achievement. These competing values produced a mixture of these motives in players. As with any individual or team, diverse motives are present. In the end Wyllie's 1991 World Cup team, which was co-coached with John Hart, was full of tension. It was destined not to succeed because of the power and rivalry that existed.

While all the recent coaches of the All Blacks have had outstanding provincial records, Laurie Mains is probably the one who best translated his knowledge and skill as a coach to the international level. He raised the skills of the All Blacks and built on the conditioning methods Alex Wyllie had introduced. Main's analysis of games and training methods were in advance of what other coaches were doing with international sides. A poisoned chalice robbed him of the possibility of winning the World Cup. Food poisoning two days before the final caused players to perform below their potential. New Zealanders will remember the heroic way the All Blacks played and only lost with the Joel Stransky drop goal near the end of extra time. Their spirit so captured the nation that they were given a ticker tape parade up Queen St in Auckland. Mains' legacy was a large group of test-hardened All Blacks, players he had developed to the highest standards.

After failing to be selected as All Black coach twice, John Hart was finally able to fulfil his ambitions. Perhaps he should have been appointed earlier – when he was at the peak of his success. He had been a controversial figure with an outstanding provincial coaching record. His early successes as All Black coach over Scotland and Australia, followed by a series win in South Africa and tri-nations championship were highlights. It lifted him to new heights. He had successfully made the transition to international rugby and professional coaching and had set up structures and systems for the new era. What followed were five straight defeats, which had never before happened in the history of the All Blacks. Condemnation then followed the loss in the World Cup to France. It may not have been the loss as much as the lacklustre performance of the side that caused such a reaction. They followed this with a spiritless game against the Springboks in the play-off. Players found the structure and systems imposed by Hart were stifling. It was as if his early success had led to over-controlling, and this was his downfall.

Wayne Smith and John Mitchell have come to the All Blacks from professional coaching backgrounds. Disappointing results marked Smith's tenure. This could have been averted had it not been for two games where Australia scored last-second tries. Other than that, he would have had wins in the Bledisloe Cup and tri-nations championship. This highlights how fine the margin is between success and failure. His difficulties were in dealing with the expectations of the media and the Rugby Union. The expectation was, and is, that the team always has to be winners. This created too much pressure and he resigned. John Mitchell showed ability as Super Twelve coach of the Waikato Chiefs and has international experience as the assistant coach with England. This knowledge and experience now has to be transferred into All Black rugby.

Leadership and motivation

In international rugby the intensity of the need to win places enormous pressure on the coach. In New Zealand we have been used to winning because of a great dedication by players and coaches to the game. Other nations could not easily match our standard. With the introduction of professionalism, they quickly caught up and our expectations have to be adjusted to the fact that these other nations now have similar levels of dedication and skill.

While focusing on winning is largely accepted, it is not an effective predictor of achievement in sport. Those who come out ahead in competitive situations focus on performance excellence rather than on the end result of winning. John Mitchell is inheriting an attitude that says you had better not lose. This attitude inhibits the ability to excel and it will hold our All Black team back unless a significant shift takes place in New Zealand's rugby psyche. John Kirwan has said, 'I'm sure that the negative motivation of fear of losing, which the All Blacks have often used, is a bad thing.'[5]

If we look at Peter Blake, he could be called our most unsuccessful yachtsman. He competed in five around-the-world races before he won the Whitbread, he made two Jules Verne attempts in a catamaran before setting the record, and he also had a failure before winning the America's Cup. Failure to him was not a sign of a lack of progress. He could accept setbacks. His old crew still celebrate annually their dismasting in the first around-the-world yacht race. He didn't see it as a disaster, but rather battled on. From all this he learnt and triumphed and became one of our most notable sailors. The enjoyment of challenge drove him on. We need more of this spirit in rugby.

Reading what All Black coaches have written on motivation reminds me of Professor Beaglehole's comment on Captain Cook: 'Never did a man write so much and reveal so little about himself.'

Never have coaches said so much and revealed so little about how they motivate players. Wyllie felt that the chemistry of a successful team could never be fully analysed. As a coach he knew that 'you can tell when it feels right, and you can tell when it feels wrong.' What he found hard was 'turning wrong to right.' With all his experience as a player and coach, he felt that judging the pre-game feeling was something that was still difficult. 'You go around and look at the players in the dressing room; you wonder, are they there? Are they ready to go? Have they built themselves up? You can go and yell and scream at them and slap them on the back, but the experts say that only lasts ten minutes. It has to be within them, and the build-up might have started a long way back.' Trying to understand what happens to his players before a game has often occupied Wyllie's mind. He still has no concrete answer and says, 'Anyone who could work out why a group feels good one day, and not the next, would be a millionaire.'[6]

Most rugby jocks react negatively to the distinction I make about putting the concern for excellence ahead of winning. Oddly enough, players in the Canterbury team say that winning wasn't the start and finish of Wyllie's approach to rugby. According to Phil Gifford, biographer of Alex Wyllie, winning wasn't a thought that would automatically spring to Wyllie's mind. Captain Don Hayes found out how serious Wyllie was about quality of performance: 'We'd played Fiji in the last game of the South Pacific tournament and we won it, and won the championship. Alex was really shitty. You'd have thought we'd lost the Ranfurly Shield. It took half the night to talk him around a bit, but he wouldn't concede that we deserved the title, because we'd played it wrong.'[7]

When the Canterbury team was down 24–0 at halftime in the great Ranfurly Shield defence against Auckland, Wyllie wasn't angry – he was sorry for them: 'They weren't losing with dignity.' In his famous short talk, he grabbed the ball and said, 'Look, they scored their points with this, so can you.' As Victor Simpson, who was in the team, said, 'If he had pounded us, that would have sent us straight down the tubes.' While quality rugby was important to Wyllie, he became more aware that as All Black coach it was probably better to play scrappy rugby and win than to play good rugby and lose. The unpleasant reality was the New Zealand Rugby Union demanded victories. He wanted the team to play quality rugby and believed the winning would come.[8]

Wyllie's approach to coaching was to start with the basics and build from that foundation. He would tell players to forget the moves until they could make fast and accurate passes without dropping the ball. He would then gradually bring in some simple moves, like bringing in the fullback and missing him with the pass. By the time he had finished they had some moves that were pretty sophisticated. He noted that 'You don't go out coaching and tell your players what they do in every situation. I've seen some jokers do that, but it turns your players into robots, and that's not achieving anything.' He believed that as a coach 'You should be trying to encourage them to think under pressure, playing their own game, and doing the right things at different times. You put ideas into them, discuss things, give some advice, say when things went right, say where they took a wrong option.'[9]

Laurie Mains was heavily influenced by Vic Cavanagh. After his third game of senior rugby, he was invited to Cavanagh's office at the Otago Daily Times and told he needed to sharpen his reactions. Cavanagh noted that Mains didn't know enough about forward play. Being a fullback, Mains wondered what he was on about. Cavanagh impressed on him the need to understand what the forwards were doing – to be able to pick when they were likely to win the ball so he could move into an attacking position. He should be able to do this by judging the way the ruck was being formed. He needed to do this if he was to anticipate moves and be in a good position. In the end, Mains said, he could read the opposition plays. He knew when the first-five was intending to run, pass, place a wipers kick or drop a kick into the box. He could read this by the way a first-five stood. That afternoon in Vic Cavanagh's office prompted Mains to start analysing players and plays. This knowledge was one of the assets he brought to his coaching.

The motivational approach Mains brought to teams can only be deduced indirectly from what he has to say about rugby. In his preparation for the World Cup he had four training camps, and examining these provides some insight into the way he went about conditioning players mentally as well as physically. Strategy was obviously a prominent feature, along with physical training methods. He used a number of fitness specialists, sprint coaches, experts in aerobic fitness: 'Everything to get the edge.' Sport psychologists were rejected because he concluded that 'Most All Blacks are such strong, independent people they didn't need them. A little bit of guidance on goal setting was probably enough for most of them.'[10] Rod Macqueen, on the other hand, did call on the advice of a sport psychologist for his Australian World Cup winning team. He found it useful to have someone looking at his performance and the dynamics of the team.

In all fairness to Laurie Mains, most sport psychology relates to developing the attitudes of finely tuned athletes in individual sports who have to peak for only a few events in a year. Rugby players are more like commandos who need to be rugged and prepared for arduous physical activity on a regular basis. The coach, however, does need to understand sport psychology. This is the premise of this book. The coach's leadership and motivation of players is the impetus for creating a successful team. The greater the understanding in this area the more effective a coach can become.

In the training camps, Mains' attention to detail, his high standards, and the training programme he devised built confidence and skill. This is where the seeds of excellence were sown. Players were motivated to attain a high level of physical and mental fitness so that they could take on and beat the rest of the world. It was not only Mains' attention to the team as a whole but also the individual attention he gave players that made a difference. For example, a young Andrew Mehrtens had never received instruction on kicking techniques to ensure consistency where he punted the ball, until taught by Mains. It was not only his knowledge of back play that earned respect. Colin Meads considered him a brilliant technical coach of forwards.

In Mains' biography his philosophy of rugby is quoted as one where 'A great deal of purpose and activity is going on, that creates pressure on the opposition by retention of the ball and the speed with which manoeuvres and moves are carried out, that opposition defences cannot keep regrouping to stop us scoring.'[11] Technically he saw everything being done right. Everyone knew what to do in each situation. This was brought about by showing each player a hundred different situations, not so that he knew a hundred different things, but by building a basic philosophy so that the player could make his own competent decisions when needed. This expectation of player performance requires individual confidence and self-knowledge. It is about gaining the initiative and building motivation. Mains devised a way of translating this attitude into the team practice. He astutely combined his practical knowledge of rugby with the dimensions that build achievement thinking.

In his book, John Hart reveals little about his coaching style and how he motivates players. He was credited with man-management skills from his role as Corporate Human Resources Manager at Fletcher Challenge. He is a high achiever and his professional management background helped him to encourage the development of players. His make-up included a very competitive mentality. His competitive behaviour as a player initially raised concerns about his ability to adapt to being a coach. As a player he was known for mouthing off at the opposition to put them off. 'As a club coach I ranted and raved. It was an extension of my playing. That sort of attitude can be successful in club rugby but the higher you go the more circumspect you have to be.'[12]

Andy Haden noted, 'Hart motivated by manipulation.' This is a very competitive style. He said, 'Hart found out why guys were playing and how to turn their reasons to his advantage. There are the traditional rugby types who will play come hell or high water. They will walk over broken glass to play. Those guys are easy for the Alex Wyllie-type coach. He can abuse and threaten them. But what about the guy who it doesn't work with? Hart had the ability to get the best out of that type as well. That was his strength.' Because of the way he motivated individuals through manipulation, Haden wondered if Auckland were a team in the sense that sides of the past were. He felt that Hart's method of motivating was effective if the team was skilled, but it was not beneficial to the team to have a lot of individuals looking after themselves. Similarly, Mike Brewer noted that Hart's style of generating competition between team members motivated them, but it could also knock a player's self-confidence. He felt that is what happened to the 1999 World Cup side. Hart himself says that developing team spirit and camaraderie was not a primary concern of his. It was what happened on the field that counted.

Leadership styles

It is possible to analyse recent All Black coaches' styles of leadership from their writings, media comments and other recollections of their behaviour. These coaches are usually a combination of the styles that have been outlined previously. They generally have a primary style supplemented by one or two back-up styles. At times they may display a wider range of behaviours than these styles suggest but usually their behaviour is consistent with a narrower range of deeply held beliefs. In analysing recent All Black coaches, I will focus on their most significant styles. It can be said that they were all high on achievement and, to varying degrees, perfectionism. Insisting on extremely high standards and getting the detail right almost becomes an obsession at international level. This perfectionism creates tension and burnout. This is one of the main reasons coaches need to be replaced. The pressure is on when making a mistake can lose a test match and all the angst that causes.

Hart was very competitive in his coaching style. Competitiveness in a coach can lead to a preoccupation with manipulating others to get what he wants. It can also arise from wanting to be admired and be the centre of attention. Competitiveness leads to jealousy and envy when others are more successful. Rather than work co-operatively to achieve a goal, competitive coaches tend to work against others in the hope of emerging as 'superior'. They can become so preoccupied with this that they lose sight of their values and beliefs. This not only limits their effectiveness, but also jeopardises the quality and effectiveness of the team they are coaching. Politics and power became entwined with Hart's desire to achieve. In many ways the great potential and eventual failure of John Hart as a coach was due to his power and competitiveness, which gave him the drive to win, but in the end was at the expense of his ability to manage a team that could continue to excel.

Wyllie was achievement and power oriented. As he matured as a coach the power style declined, except when he came under pressure to win later in his All Black coaching career. In the end his anger and frustration affected his ability to cope with the stress associated with being an All Black coach.

Mains was achievement-oriented with a high degree of perfectionism. He was known to prepare meticulously for training sessions. He could also be a little distant from his players and was initially hard to get to know, which is a characteristic of a perfectionist. It was his conscientious applications and well thought-out strategies in training which gained players' respect.

Wayne Smith was also a constructive oriented coach. Unlike Hart and Wyllie, where power and competitiveness were the potholes in their psyches, Smith may have lacked the necessary levels of these aggressive styles. A certain level of assertiveness and competitiveness is necessary in an international coach. The degree of influence each of the various styles has is what is important when considering the effectiveness of a coach. When power is expressed as respect for the chain of command, loyalty and forcefulness, it is quite functional in a team. When the behaviour is too prominent and becomes controlling, dictatorial and aggressive it creates disharmony. Similarly, competitive behaviour has its place when it is self-assertive and creates a healthy comparison of self to others. It becomes destructive when competition takes over from co-operation and develops opponents rather than allies.

Laurie Mains had the most constructive coaching style. Competitive and power motivation were not excessive. He had a very high achievement orientation. This gave him strong cause-and-effect thinking and the ability to analyse problems and create excellence. His perfectionism didn't interfere with this skill, although his emotional distance may have caused him to lack some of the intensity necessary to motivate a team in the few days he had available before a home test match. On tour or with time to prepare a team his achievement style won through. He has since been able to go on to other successes in his post-All Black career with teams in South Africa and again with Otago.

All these coaches were innovative in some way – Smith with defence, Wyllie in developing superior fitness in his team which gave them the advantage towards the end of a game, Hart in the dynamic attacking style of rugby he developed and Mains in using the 'pick up and go' as a new strategy to counter opposition forwards fringing the rucks. They all had successful provincial coaching records. All were good organisers and paid attention to detail. All were achievement-oriented. Power and competitive motives interfered with the success of Wyllie and Hart. Smith struggled with the pressures of the job and needed more self-confidence. The step up to being the All Black coach is a monumental one. Jim Bolger remarked, 'I'd like to be All Black coach when they win, but I'm glad I'm Prime Minister when they lose.'[13]

Laurie Mains was the most effective of the New Zealand coaches that have been discussed. However, a coach who has really stood out, and has had the most success, is Australian Rod Macqueen. He coached the Wallabies to wins in the Tri-Nations series and the Bledisloe Cup, brought home the World Cup and beat the Lions in a test series. Before that he coached the NSW Waratahs, was the first coach for the ACT Brumbies and led this team of rejected players from the other two states to semi-final and final slots in the two years he coached. It was his organisational ability and approach to coaching that created this success and led to his selection as Wallabies coach.

Vision, organisation and attention to detail were the hallmarks of Macqueen's approach to coaching. At club level he was able to take a second division side to the top by creating a vision for the whole club. All the coaches in the club were brought into that vision and teams throughout the grades used the same basic moves and tactics. This involved all teams practising the same moves and formalising defensive and attacking patterns. Putting these pieces in place gave a structure and platform to develop players not only as a team but also as a whole club dedicated to improving performance. The fine line was making sure that it didn't impede innovation, individualism and the spontaneity of the players and coaches.

Innovation was another of the outstanding qualities Macqueen brought to the role. The way he coached the Brumbies reflected his belief in encouraging a new and different style of play. To achieve this, he involved his players in the training process by seeking their advice and input. He believed that by including people in the decision making process 'You are much more likely to get a result that is supported and works. Additionally, those who are involved in the decision-making are able to see when things go wrong and therefore are able to help solve the problem.'[14]

Macqueen believed that success on the field would come only if player bonding and team spirit were continually boosted. The trademark of his coaching was commitment, organisation and discipline. Fitness was obviously addressed but far more important was commitment and attitude. This passion was not the type of ranting heard in some dressing rooms before a game. Passion to Macqueen is 'something that needs to be built over a long period of time, it needs a foundation and needs to mature and to be nurtured.'[15] To develop this camaraderie and positive attitude he used player input to establish firm guidelines and principles so the players became self-regulating.

'Rod certainly has tremendous man-management skills as well as an outstanding rugby mind,'[16] says Brumbies captain Brett Robinson. It is interesting that in his book Macqueen does not credit himself with having great technical skills but rather the ability to comprehend the pattern of a game and to manage and motivate a team. He drew on others to help with the technical aspects and expected the players to work things out together. This is in contrast to some of the expectations on All Black coaches, where technical mastery is viewed as highly important. Nearly every All Black coach has played as an All Black. This has not been the case in Australia, where more emphasis has been placed on management and motivation ability.

Macqueen believed that while his management style was efficient it could also drive a lot of people mad. 'My insistence on leaving no stone unturned to give the players and management the best possible preparation meant I was constantly checking and rechecking what was to be done. In retrospect I could see that sometimes I would go over the top.'[17] Because he encouraged free and open discussion, people could make positive suggestions about his coaching or air any grievances. From this feedback he learned to modify his style. 'There is no doubt that at times I became too dictatorial and things would start to go wrong before I was able to realise it. I have often found myself in that position throughout my career and when able to recognise the situation, or at least be alerted to it, I have tried to make the necessary changes to move forward.'[18]

In relating Macqueen's coaching to the leadership styles, he can be described as high achievement, creative and encouraging. He is also a perfectionist. The constructive styles he possesses counter-balance this to a great extent. These are similar qualities to those of Laurie Mains, except Macqueen is more extroverted by nature and passionate in expressing his feelings. They both had the objective of creating a team in which selflessness was the primary driving force.

Professional rugby now has full-time players and needs a new breed of coach. It is not just the on-field work that they must be able to manage. Such coaches have to continuously supervise players and manage other coaching staff and a medical team. They have to take into account player recruitment, media comments and responsibility to sponsors. They need to plan well ahead, develop ongoing strategies and study the opposition for strengths and weaknesses in order to develop a game plan.

Coaching a national side places a person under a harsh spotlight. The media and the public believe they have the right to criticise. The coach is under scrutiny in public life. Such pressure is considerable. We need to change the expectations that we have of the coach and learn that 'sometimes losing games helps to develop passion and a belief in working harder' – not my words, but Rod Macqueen's. We should be looking to improve standards and the pursuit of excellence, rather than just winning and losing.

Having full-time professional coaches and players changes the approach to training. Everything they do, from weights in the gymnasium to their consumption of food, is supervised. This is in contrast to the amateur game. There are, however, lessons that can be learned by the amateur coach. It is like knowledge from Formula One racing that the ordinary driver can pick up and use. The same motivational and leadership skills needed in coaching a professional team apply at the amateur level.

Summary

This chapter examined the strategies and styles employed by coaches at international level. The leadership style of the coaches was paramount when examining their effectiveness. This related to how they motivated and managed players. Their ways of operating were contrasted to achievement, encouraging, perfectionistic, competitive and power styles. It showed that the more effective coaches were strongly achievement and encouragement oriented. They were able to balance the task demands of being a coach with a concern for players through the values they held and the leadership strategies they used. They were innovative and involved their players. This formed the basis for building successful teams.

I am indebted to Paul Verdon for his background work on All Black coaches. His book The Power Behind The All Blacks *tells the previously untold story of the men who coached the All Blacks. Some material has been taken directly from his book and Verdon's comments provide useful insights into the contributions these coaches made.*

1. Paul Verdon, *The Power Behind The All Blacks*
2. Paul Verdon, *The Power Behind The All Blacks*
3. Paul Verdon, *The Power Behind The All Blacks*
4. Paul Verdon, *The Power Behind The All Blacks*
5. Ken Hodge and Alex McKenzie, *Thinking Rugby*
6. Phil Gifford, *Grizz: The Legend*
7. Phil Gifford, *Grizz: The Legend*
8. Phil Gifford, *Grizz: The Legend*
9. Phil Gifford, *Grizz: The Legend*
10. Bob Howitt and Robin McConnell, *Laurie Mains*
11. Bob Howitt and Robin McConnell, *Laurie Mains*
12. Joseph Romano, *Making Of Champions, Great NZ Coaches*
13. Paul Verdon, *The Power Behind The All Blacks*
14. Rod Macqueen, *One Step Ahead*
15. Rod Macqueen, *One Step Ahead*
16. Rod Macqueen, *One Step Ahead*
17. Rod Macqueen, *One Step Ahead*
18. Rod Macqueen, *One Step Ahead*

Chapter 6

LESSONS FROM AMERICAN SPORTS COACHES

We can learn a lot from American coaches. I have found that the books written by New Zealand coaches reveal little about their coaching philosophies. This may reflect the fact that we have only just moved into the professional era, whereas in the US coaching has been a professional occupation for a long time. Take someone like Don Shula, previously the coach of the Miami Dolphins. He had 18 assistant coaches, a squad of 50 to 60 players and ran a front office that had a turnover of millions of dollars. His background included playing football and getting a degree at university, then coaching college football, being an assistant coach in the professional franchise and finally becoming head coach. This gave him a lifetime of experience in coaching and motivating players. Coaches with this sort of background are more articulate about motivation because they have been heavily involved in sophisticated coaching situations that call on sports science and management theory. This is only just starting to happen in New Zealand.

To develop the theme that has been set out so far, I have researched American coaches and identified the advice they have given about achievement, encouraging, competitive and power coaching behaviours. These comments are set out below and I appreciate having permission to quote these coaches. The coaches quoted are listed on the following page:

Basketball

Phil Jackson

Coached the Chicago Bulls for three successive NBA championships and then the Los Angeles Lakers to NBA success.

Pat Riley

Coached the Los Angeles Lakers to four championship titles in nine years.

John Wooden

Was UCLA's legendary coach and one of the most successful college basketball coaches in the history of the game.

Football

Don Shula

Was head coach and led the Miami Dolphins to five Super Bowl appearances and the Baltimore Colts to one. He has been the 'winningest' coach in NFL history.

Lou Holtz

Revitalised the Notre Dame football team, as head coach, by leading them to nine bowl games and a national championship.

Vince Lombardi

A legend in pro-football as the head coach of the Green Bay Packers 1960–68.

Other football head coaches quoted are **Marty Schottenheimer**, Kansas City Chiefs; **Darrell Royal**, University of Texas Longhorns; **Woody Hayes**, of Ohio State University; and **Dennis Green**, of the Minnesota Vikings.

Achievement values

Challenge	We made a stretching beyond present levels of success both a habit and a system. – Pat Riley
Positive approach	I've always used a player's accomplishments rather than his failures to weigh his potential. – Lou Holtz
Constructive	The doer makes mistakes and I want doers on my team – players who make things happen. – John Wooden
Attitude to mistakes	When they made a mistake, they'd look over at the bench. I immediately cut them off. 'Why are you looking at me?' I'd ask. 'You already knew you made a mistake.' – Phil Jackson
Seeks all available information	Coach never gave the impression that he knew everything. That was his greatest strength as a coach. – Denny Crun on John Wooden
Personal responsibility	Woody [Hayes] didn't like to impose rules, and he laboured to build up an attitude toward commonly held goals and values to lessen the need for rules. – Gary Walton (biographer)
Goals	I identify concrete objectives that I feel our team has at least a 70–75% chance of success. I don't make them too low, because why aim low? I don't want to put them out of sight either. Players know the difference. If goals aren't set properly, they lose meaning. – Marty Schottenheimer

Best of ability	My belief is you win with good people. I've had a number of people who, on the surface, didn't possess great ability but who exhibited outstanding character and tremendous motivation. – Don Shula
	Some of our best players were considered marginal athletes at one time. But I wanted them on the team because they gave every ounce of their ability every time they walked on the field. – Denis Green
Standards of performance	As a team we set standards which we thought would make us a championship team. As a group we monitored each other. As coach I enforced them. This moment transformed me as a coach. I've never changed back. – Pat Riley
	Over the years, I have become convinced that every detail is important and that success usually accompanies attention to little details. It is this, in my judgement, that makes the difference between champion and near champion. – John Wooden
Push beyond the limits	As coach you have to ask performers to go beyond themselves, to push their limits. – Don Shula
Think for themselves	At the core of my vision was getting the players to think for themselves . . . I had to give them the freedom to find out what worked and what didn't. – Phil Jackson

Direct and honest	If team members aren't giving their best, I think that situation has to be confronted straight on. – Don Shula
Concentrate on fundamentals	He reduced complexities to essentials, making the game easier to learn. He wanted simple things done with consistent excellence rather than complicated things done poorly. – Journalist William Furlong on Vince Lombardi
	I have observed people so frustrated by failure, they abandon the fundamentals that brought them success. – Lou Holtz
Excellence	You knew immediately that Lombardi was a dedicated individual, sincere and possessed of a burning desire to succeed, and that he would accept nothing other than the best efforts of everyone. – Kramer (player)
	You must possess something inside of yourself that eschews mediocrity. – Lou Holtz
Feedback	Feedback is the breakfast of champions, but it can only be given effectively in an environment where people don't feel they have to defend themselves all the time. – Don Shula
Review performance	Each week we had goals based on what we need to do to win that particular game. Then each Monday, we go over the results – we met this goal – good job. We didn't meet this one. All right, we know what we have to work on. – Marty Schottenheimer

Encouraging values

Recognition of performance	Recognising good performance is an important part of my coaching. – Don Shula
Team rituals	We started and ended each practice in a circle to symbolise that we were forming our own sacred hoop. – Phil Jackson
Concern for others	Creating a caring atmosphere is not a complex task. Simply follow the golden rule to treat others as you want to be treated. When you concern yourself about the welfare of others you engender loyalty and respect. – Lou Holtz
Resolve conflict constructively	When I saw the team's incohesiveness, I should have done everything I could to discover the cause. I should have called a team meeting . . . and announced that no one was leaving until we had uncovered the problem. – Lou Holtz
Encouraging and supportive	You want to support people when they're first learning, then gradually get more choosy about when you give them praise. – Don Shula
Understanding individuals	One of the remarkable features about Lombardi was his capacity to understand players as individuals. – Michael O'Brien (biographer)
Respect for others	When I get upset it is always focused on performance. Respect for my team members is a given. – Don Shula

Power values

Domineering	There was a time when a leader could get results by saying, 'Do this because I say so.' That approach falls flat today. – Marty Schottenheimer
Controlling	Some coaches feel threatened when their players start exerting their independence. They keep a tight rein on everyone and set strict guidelines on how each person should perform. That approach may work in isolated cases but it actually only creates resentment, particularly with the new breed of players who are more independent than their predecessors. – Phil Jackson
Fear	Fear of failure will lead you towards despair, wrong decisions and incomplete performance. – Pat Riley
Aggressive	Compassion is vital. Without it, anger degenerates into brutality and tears the fabric of the team. As much as possible, a positive emotional environment has to govern the team. – Pat Riley

While there are examples of aggressive coaches being successful such reports are often exaggerated. Don Shula, head coach of the Miami Dolphins, says, 'All this talk that coaches are effective when they're toughest and most demanding is just an impression that has been developed through the national media.'

Competitive values

Egotistical	What tears a team apart is when players develop the 'Disease of Me' and an over-powering belief in their own importance. They try to prove that they really are as important as the fawning press and idolising fans think. – Pat Riley
Win/lose mentality	My obsession with winning was often my undoing. That lesson was an important turning point for me. – Phil Jackson Win or die was the code. But that kind of approach, though it often gets the players' juices flowing, interferes with concentration and ultimately backfires. – Phil Jackson
Comparing individuals to each other	We had always ranked a player's performance against that of his teammates until someone pointed out that these comparisons were self-defeating. – Pat Riley
Unrealistic challenges	If you blindly take on challenges beyond your level of preparation, you saddle your team with avoidable disappointment. – Pat Riley
False confidence	False confidence, however, can be worse than no confidence. I would never inflate an athlete's ego by making him think he was more talented than he was. Tell a player he's outstanding and he will be demoralised when he discovers he isn't. – Lou Holtz

Personal values

The following statements capture some of the key themes outlined in this book. They highlight the fact that coaching is a values-oriented role. Possessing the constructive attitudes and values oneself is the starting point for leading and motivating others. Coaches expressed these ideas:

> I'd say that in the long run, winning coaching has more to do with the coach's own beliefs. – Don Shula

> It's the coach's – the leader's – beliefs that are most important; they become self-fulfilling. – Don Shula

> It would not be an exaggeration to say that how a team plays tells you something about the coach. – Darryl Sutter

> Winners and losers aren't born, they are the products of how they think. – Lou Holtz

> Wooden's remarkable success stemmed primarily from his values and his consistency in living by those values. – Gary Walton (Biographer)

Summary

In this chapter, quotes have been taken from leading US football and basketball coaches that highlight the important attitudes, beliefs and values that underlie effective coaching. Training under coaches like these brings out the best in players. In order to convey these values to team members, coaches must hold these views themselves and be able to communicate them effectively.

Phil Jackson and Hugh Delehanty, *Sacred Hoops*
Pat Riley, *The Winner Within*
John Wooden with Jack Tobin, *They Call Me Coach*
Don Shula and Ken Blanchard, *Everyone's A Coach*
Lou Holtz, *Winning Every Day*
Michael O'Brien, *Vince*
Ray Didinger (ed.), *Game Plans For Success*
Gary M Walton, *Beyond Winning*

Chapter 7

APPROACH TO TRAINING

There needs to be a mentality in the team that espouses excellence. This means developing in every player the desire to excel. Selection is the initial step in the process. This can be a trial game, picking players on past performance or judging them at practice. Usually it is a combination of all three. Another important aspect to consider is what attitudes the individual players hold and how they will contribute to the team. After selection, the first step is developing individual effectiveness. This begins with physical and mental conditioning. There is also a need to reinforce achievement values at this stage. In the last chapter, Lombardi was quoted as never accepting anything other than the best effort from everyone. That is the starting point.

Standard of performance

Setting standards of performance gives players a clear view of what has to be done to achieve team goals. The quote by Pat Riley in the previous chapter outlined how he and his team set and monitored standards that they thought would make them a champion team. This method transformed him as a coach. This highlights the importance of setting and monitoring standards. Lou Holtz similarly reinforced this point saying, 'The standards you set yourself are a real measure of your dedication. The greater your commitment to excellence, the higher the standards you'll be willing to accept.' There needs to be a high level of expectation but standards should also be realistic. They should be clearly communicated and encourage players to set individual goals regarding their level of performance. It is a matter of being optimistic about what players can attain. Such expectations need to be established jointly. This means determining what needs to be done to accomplish a particular goal.

There should always be a certain amount of challenge involved in reaching these goals. Breaking them down into standards of performance gives players a clearer picture of what they must do in order to get there. The probability of attaining the goals should be linked to skill, not chance. In other words, if the team is able to perform to certain standards of skill and put in place the desired patterns of play, then it should be able to achieve the overall goals that have been set. Motivation comes from emphasising the satisfaction of accomplishing these standards and goals.

Generally, the greater the goal difficulty, while still being attainable, the higher the level of performance attained. Further, it has been found that the effort taken to achieve goals is greater when feedback is provided on performance. Also, the more specific the standards, the more effort and persistence is put into attaining the desired result. However, if the goals are too difficult there is more variability in performance. Low achievers will persist with impossible goals. High achievers are more likely to withdraw and reassess. The opposite is the case when the goal is difficult but attainable. High achievers are most motivated when attaining their goal has about a 50/50 chance of success. It is then that they feel their effort will make the difference. Generally they set goals that are attainable through hard work.

The greatest statement Captain Cook ever made about himself was to do with standards. After plunging into the Southern Ocean to try to find the southern continent that geographers thought was there and coming up against the ice pack of the Antarctic, he said, 'I have not gone as far as any other man, but as far as a man may go.' He didn't set his standards on beating others but what was possible for him to achieve.

The attainment of specific and challenging standards results in more satisfaction for the achiever than the attainment of easy or vague standards. Standards that are considered most important or consistent with the goals of the team should have the greatest focus. Each member of the team needs to decide how he can contribute to the team goals through the standard of performance he sets himself. Discussing what is expected of each other heightens commitment and the will to work together. Bill Walsh, an American football coach, believed that players establish a standard of performance over time. 'There is a bonding, a pride that develops within a winning team, so the coach may not even be the one who demands the standard. The players will demand it of each other.'[1]

The coach needs to talk to each player about his personal standards and goals. Then he or she must monitor progress, provide feedback and make the necessary modifications. Keep in mind that goals need to be revisited and aligned with the reality of the situation. Continual clarification is needed about the standards of performance required. As the team progresses the standards need to be lifted. This is the process of continuous improvement. These relate to fitness, strength, skills and performance on the field.

Physical and mental conditioning

Players need to be told that the fundamental value they can provide the team comes from giving their best. This is the criterion for selection that needs to be communicated and demonstrated at practice. One example involves taking the squad to a sharp rise or slope beside the practice field. Their task is to run 20–25 metres to the top as hard as they can – 'their best effort'. Then down to the bottom and do it again. Repeat it another four or five times, each time emphasising that it has to be their best effort. If anyone doesn't give their best, tell them it won't be counted and immediately do it again. They will be getting fairly breathless. Tell them that they have to do it one more time – give their best – it will be the last time. Invariably they do give it a real effort, but don't accept it – saying, 'It isn't good enough'. Then 'One more time and give your best'. Then, again and again, repeat the exercise. This really becomes punishing. You are now starting to push them beyond their limits. It is really making them pull something out of themselves. This really tests their endurance both physically and mentally. About this time you admit what you are doing isn't fair but it is a test of their determination not to quit.

Rugby does require players to dig deep within themselves. They can be on attack and then seconds later be defending their line because of a break-down in play. That requires the same fortitude that is developed on 'the hill.' It is relatively easy to see those who buy into this challenge and will not give in. It is a quality that coach Denis Green noted made some of his best players. At one stage they were marginal members of his squad but because they gave their best every time they walked onto a field their ability improved. When players are giving their best, their skills invariably rise.

Working 'the hill' becomes a 'love-hate' affair with the team. They know it draws something out of them that has an extra special dimension. Lombardi would push his players to the end of their endurance and then beyond it, and if there was some reserve, he found that too. Going up that hill as fast as they can, and not knowing how many times it is going to be repeated, calls on a spirit in players that personifies determination. It is at times necessary to push players beyond what they think are their physical and psychological boundaries. It is emphasised that such training focuses on lifting the standard of players' mental and physical ability. It is not a sadistic form of punishment. The frequency with which the exercise is used should not be overdone, otherwise it will lose some of its effectiveness.

It has been interesting to watch the reactions to 'the hill' training over the years. Generally, I believe that practice should be an enjoyable experience. 'The hill' is something that is largely outside this principle. I first learnt this exercise when going through selection for the SAS during National Service. It was gut-wrenching stuff and more punishing than the level suggested for rugby training. It did, however, bring something out of you that provided a remarkable experience. It confronted you with your own determination and will to keep going. These are essential qualities in a rugby player. John Hart took the All Blacks on an SAS training camp to provide them with that experience.

I have found 'the hill' to be an excellent selection method for finding out who is going to give their best. One year there was a young man who was experiencing difficulties getting up 'the hill.' Everyone was at the top and he was only half way up and struggling. I could see he was trying and gave him encouragement. Once he got to the top we all went down again and repeated the exercise. Good on him for trying to give his best. We could always help him to get fitter but the determination and spirit he was showing was something that came from within and only he could produce. Later the teacher whom I was helping in coaching the team told me that the young man was having a mild asthma attack and was finding it hard to breathe. Because I was encouraging him as he struggled up 'the hill' and he was not too distressed, the teacher didn't interfere. That player became the captain and what an example he set the team. Once, when they were down 17 points at half-time, he said, 'Now you know why we run up and down that bloody hill.' They turned the game around.

I was reluctant to use 'the hill' training for junior grades as it is very punishing and, I felt, inappropriate at their level. One day at practice, after my under 10-year-olds had played poorly, I decided to give them a little shake-up by introducing 'the hill.' They loved it! Up they would go and all would come sliding down on the wet grass, it was great fun. I get secondary school teams to do 'the hill' at some, but not all, of their practices. Once I was approached by senior boys who suggested that 'the hill' was too punishing for a junior team I was helping to coach. Fortunately at that very moment one of the milder mannered boys in the team came up and said, 'Please sir, can we do "the hill" now?'

Those who can't hack 'the hill' won't make the team. Surprisingly few have fallen into this category. Usually they drift away rather than get dropped. The team is not for them. Some of the most impressive players have come from the B squads. They struggle up 'the hill' because they may not have the same physical prowess as the top players but know that giving their best is a standard that they can meet. It creates a whole new purpose for them in sport. With the right atmosphere and encouragement, most try hard and achieve their standard. What does happen is that some players in the average range start to grow in stature as the season progresses. Once a player learns to give his best it is inevitable that an improvement in performance takes place. One who made the top team because of this quality started the season on the bench, but by the championship round he had become a dominant force in the forward pack. In the final it was emphasised that the team had to give 110 percent effort. He didn't, his was 120 percent, and he was the outstanding player of the match. That is the sort of growth and development that takes place when players learn to give their best. World champion runner John Walker said excellence was 5 percent genes and 95 percent training and determination.

Excellence – giving your best

Enticing such qualities out of players is one of the most rewarding experiences of being a rugby coach. When they learn to give their best, to push beyond their boundaries, they learn a lesson that carries through to other aspects of their lives. It is an intrinsic quality in all of us, one we are all capable of eliciting, but for many it is something that is never tapped. Learning this lesson is the start of laying the foundation for excellence. Mind you, it is not a matter of saying, 'I did my best.' I have seen groups where that was a blithe comment. It must an honest, determined and heart-felt effort. It has to be real.

To make the team, players must give their best. It is not acceptable to have someone in the team who is not willing to make that commitment. Giving your best is one thing every player can do. I would rather have a player of average ability who gave his best than a talented player who gave only 80 percent, even if the talented player was still better. When you have a team that is committed to giving their best, the team dynamics really start to gel. There can be no feeling of defeat if a team has gone out and really done its best. Selecting players who respond to the call to this commitment is fundamental in developing team spirit.

This whole approach builds a positive mentality in the team. One year the captain of one of my teams was a prop who had clubfeet. This hampered his mobility but he worked his opponent over in the scrum so hard that the other prop could hardly out-run him. He had evolved to become the captain as everyone admired his determination even though he was a bit handicapped in running. As captain he learned to reinforce the message of encouraging others to 'give their best.' The lineout thrower related how he was having trouble throwing the ball in accurately during one game. 'Last year they all bitched and moaned and that would put me off.' This time the captain came up and told him he knew he was trying his best and to keep trying. 'I tell you, next time I threw that ball in I was going to get it where they wanted.'

A good time to deliver the message about giving their best is after an easy game when the team has won by 30 points or more over a weaker team, but their performance has slipped. Often when a team leads by such a big score, their play becomes looser and their concentration declines. When you tell them that you are not happy with their performance because they let their standards slip below their best, it comes as a surprise. It emphasises the point. Then when they come off after a loss and gave their best, you can talk with pride about their performance because they have met or exceeded their standards. That's when they really appreciate and understand the satisfaction gained from achievement motivation.

These sentiments are reiterated by Wayne Bennett, the Bronco's coach, when he says to players: 'The greatest challenge is getting the best out of yourself *every time* you go into a competition. The thing about winning and losing is that you can win and give a mediocre effort and you can still lose after giving it everything you have. I know which effort I'd be more proud of.'[2] To him sport is about giving it everything – which, he believes, is how you learn. Often parents asked him for advice about their kids who are just starting out in sport. Apart from the obvious fun factor, he tells them to teach their kids to be competitors. Not to quit. Not to give in. To judge themselves not on what others do but on whether or not they've given everything.

As a general rule, I tell players in the squad that if they go out and play to the best of their ability, they won't be dropped even if there is a better player on the bench. They get the message about giving their best. Players do have to be good enough to make the squad. I have seen average players in the team go out and give more than was thought possible, and so lift the team's performance that they become permanent members on the playing side. Players quickly realise they can play to their best – 'I can do that.' This is a transformational experience. When you have players in a team that go out and play like that, no matter what the outcome of the game, they have the hearts of champions.

Giving your best is not a one-off effort. It is something that must be done week in and week out. It is a matter of psychological and physical conditioning. So, in the course of a season, players need to learn to give their best effort consistently in every game. It is enjoying the struggle or the challenge of each game. The Greeks gave laurel leaves to the victor. These faded quickly and it was on to the next challenge. For the competitive player, everything is a challenge. For the achiever, it is about enjoying the challenge.

John Wooden always told his players that they could never be truly successful or obtain peace of mind unless they had the satisfaction of knowing that they had done their best. Although he wanted them to win, he tried to convince them they always won when they did their best. Jock Hobbs endorsed that Wyllie never went crook at players who had given their best. The measure of his belief was shown in the Ranfurly Shield loss to Auckland. He gave a very productive and understanding half-time talk when they were down 24–0. 'That day he really lived up to his philosophy of not minding if we were losing as long as everyone was giving a hundred percent,' said Hobbs.[3]

Perseverance

Two experiences which stand out in my mind about the importance of perseverance came from coaching at junior level. In one pre-season game I spent my time behind our own goal posts yelling, 'don't give in, don't give in,' as the score piled up against us. And they didn't. For part of the second half we even had some of the run of play. It was a proud moment after the game to be able to say to those boys that they had honoured their commitment to give their best. They lost but were never defeated. Defeat only happens when it is accepted in the mind. Their improvement through the season was substantial and they made the semi-finals.

The other experience was having a team down 50 points at half-time against the second-to-top team in the competition. I moved my young son, who was a determined little guy, into the forward pack for the second half and he must have wrestled the ball for three quarters of the second half and kept the score down to seven-all. The next week we were to play the top team. We actually won. These young boys had found something in themselves the Saturday before and went out and played far above their perceived limits. That sort of determination really taps into the idea of doing your best. It makes coaching really worthwhile.

A story I have related to players on perseverance is about the two frogs in the bowl of cream. They couldn't jump out and kept slipping down the side of the bowl. One said it was impossible and sank to the bottom, while the other kept churning away. Finally the cream turned to butter and he jumped right out. Big front row props and tough lineout jumpers have come up to me later and said how meaningful they have found the story. They would tell me about games where they had been coming off second best but they kept thinking about the frog in the bowl of cream and kept battling away. Their perseverance paid off and they came out on top.

So, the starting point in forming a high-achievement team culture is a commitment from players to give their best. The coach must provide the leadership to create this dynamic team spirit. Successful coaches invariably use a lot of achievement language to inspire players. They use comments like, 'We can improve our effort by . . .' 'The way to lift the standard is to . . .' 'I'm confident that . . .' or 'Let's do it one more time and see if . . .' together with encouragement and positive feedback on improvement. All this becomes inculcated into the thinking and behaviour of the players. It is important that this thinking style is ingrained in the coach and should come across in a natural way.

Physical conditioning and achievement

Start communicating the achievement message in the pre-season build up, initially by concentrating on fitness improvement. What distinguishes coaches that push for excellence, apart from the way they lead and motivate players, is the way they condition players to very high standards. Physical fatigue is emotionally and mentally draining too. Too many coaches do not work their players hard enough to last the game and they are worn down by the last quarter. Pre-season training is designed to get players fit. It is up to them to meet the standards that have been set. Goals need to be established for each player's fitness level. This involves assessing the strength, speed and endurance they need in order to meet the requirements of their position. It is then a matter of keeping the standards up throughout the season so they remain in top shape. To do this an assessment should be made of their initial fitness level. This can be as crude as sending them on a five-minute run around the edge of the field and recording the distance they cover, to more scientific measures of recovery rates. Strength can be the number of press-ups or chin-ups they can do, and speed can be measured by timing them over a 50-metre sprint or how many there-and-back ten-metre repetitions they can do in a set time. If the equipment is available, more scientific measures can be recorded in the gym.

Rugby fitness has become more scientific in recent years. There is now plenty of information about the requirements for each position. Once the All Black forwards were farmers who led a rugged physical existence. Now all that strength is developed in the gym. Upper body strength has become more important at senior levels. The game is also played at a faster pace, requiring additional stamina and speed. These physical attributes can be developed in players. Ultimately they must take responsibility for themselves, but the encouragement and help of the coach is an important stimulus. After goals are set concerning the level of fitness the players need to attain, a programme should be mapped out detailing how to get there. Measurement reinforces and encourages improvement. Players get a sense of progress as the standard of their fitness improves. The social aspect of the gym is also important in helping to keep up commitment. Through this process, the underlying values of achievement and encouragement are being reinforced.

Physical conditioning and pain threshold

Rugby players do need to have a high pain threshold. Pain is subjective. Psychology experiments show that those with a background in contact sports have a higher pain threshold than others. An important part of the conditioning process is to raise this threshold. Anyone who has ever achieved in sport knows what it is like to go through the pain barrier. That experience helps make the heart of a champion. Players need to be pushed to new levels of endurance. The conditioning of rugby players differs from most Olympic athletes. While there are similarities, rugby players need to be conditioned more like SAS troopers. They need to be able to play with minor injuries and take knocks. I advocate that players shouldn't stop play for injury in a game unless it is going to be aggravated by playing on. Sure, a whack on the thigh hurts but it is just as painful if you lie on the ground or if you walk behind the forward pack. In fact, not giving in to the pain and getting up on your feet probably quickens the mental and physical recovery. A player once said of Lombardi that he had a very high pain threshold. 'Our injuries didn't worry him!'

I am not advocating a player continue with a serious injury or an injury that will be aggravated by continuing play. I am also against the idea of 'big hits' in a game. This has a popular response from fans but is something that should be discouraged, particularly at lower grades. The media tend to hype up this aspect. Playing vigorously is a part of rugby but the level of physical contact should be sensible. Charging into rucks and driving the ball up the field is all part of game and helps to gain the initiative. Conditioning players in this aspect of the game is all part of the physical preparation needed for rugby. It does require courage and physical confidence. Laying out this requirement and seeing which players are willing to put themselves on the line in a physical confrontation gives you a good idea about who will make the grade.

One way to assess who will drive into the rucks is to line two forward packs up opposite each other and drop the ball in the middle. They have to go in and get possession. This exercise soon sorts out those who are willing to put themselves on the line in a physical encounter. It is a different sort of courage from doing a 'big hit.' It is an inner fortitude in the face of risk as the opposing group is coming at you and you need to concentrate on the ball. It is the same fortitude needed to take a high kick, with tacklers close at hand. Some of the players who emerge as capable in such encounters are not necessarily the outwardly tough individuals. I was once told that the way to pick the front row was to line all the players up in front of a brick wall and tell them to run into it. The ones who questioned the instruction are immediately dropped. The ones who looked at you earnestly and asked, 'How fast, coach?' – they are your front row!

When there is not a large number of players for selection, the ability of the players can vary. It is building the confidence of the less competent players that will make the difference to how the team performs. One secondary school pupil who was a bit uncoordinated but wanted to play rugby gave his all to be in the team. He was one of the brighter pupils in the school, but had to be a 'dumb forward.' His contribution was to hit rucks. While he was rather shy and reserved, this experience brought something out of him and he found a new level of confidence. His self-esteem was heightened because he proved to himself that he could master something that was really difficult for him. This is the character-building side of rugby.

What is advocated in this section seems hard. The reality is that rugby is akin to a medieval battle without swords. As long as it is played in the right spirit it is a most exhilarating game. Being involved in a contact sport does demand toughness. There is no doubt that playing contact sport requires courage. Physical conditioning is a mentally toughening process. The belief in facing physical challenges, persisting in one's efforts and reaching higher standards of performance are some of the fine qualities engendered by rugby.

Care must be taken that the mental conditioning does not degenerate into punitive coaching. While there is the hard and tough aspect of coaching, the underlying theme should be supportive but challenging. It is being able to make players better than they thought they could be. It is being able to convince players to play beyond their expectations, to push themselves through physical and psychological barriers. Don Shula is quoted as saying that as coach you are asking performers to go beyond themselves, to push their limits. While this is punishing, it is not done in the same way as an aggressive and power-oriented coach would do it. There is a different set of values operating and players are able to distinguish the difference. The power style is extrinsic, driving and demanding. The achievement style is intrinsic, challenging and supportive. The important thing is to keep encouraging players, setting challenges and appealing to something inside them rather than imposing physical demands. As the season progresses, more emphasis can be placed on skill, team patterns and maintaining fitness levels.

Skills development

The focus after physical conditioning needs to be on assessing and developing skills. At practice and in trial matches it is possible to assess the skill and ability of players by the way they train, handle the ball and push themselves to get into the play. Skill development goes hand in hand with physical and mental conditioning. Tom Schnackenberg, navigator and designer with Team New Zealand in the America's Cup, says 'What really sustains the magic for me is a feeling that we can actually improve a lot from last time. I think that is the main thing that motivates people, both as individuals and as a team. They realise they can get a lot better, so the crew are concentrating on improving their skills as sailors and figuring out how our boats work.'

Effective learning methods to develop skills vary from player to player. For some a verbal explanation may be sufficient to understand the concept the coach wants to get across. For others it is necessary to demonstrate and run through the play to teach what is required. Successful coaches vary their teaching methods. Players learn in a number of ways. To teach a new play or move, first talk the players through it. Then walk them through the move and gradually build up their speed and precision. It surprises me that more attention is not given to diagrams. These help to explain moves or defensive patterns. In basketball and American football they are widely used to explain patterns of play.

The most important aspect of coaching skills is building the motivation of players to learn and perform the required tasks. If the coach is enthusiastic, arranges equipment and helps players to clarify the purpose for learning a skill and keeps them motivated, he has solved most of the problems of learning. In such cases players will learn even if the coach's knowledge is limited. No coach can know all the intricacies of each position. Players can review how they are performing and will make adjustments because they are keen to practise and get it right. It has always surprised me how quickly they will pick up skills if their interest is tapped. They will also practise for hours on their own to master skills once they are enthusiastic about the position in which they are playing.

Learning a skill is not about getting it right once and after that being able to perform it successfully. It is a slow continual process of practising and improvement. Previously acquired skills, such as ball/eye/hand co-ordination skills in cricket or tennis, can contribute to faster learning in catching and passing a rugby ball. The previously learned skills may flow into the new situation. Children do learn many of these basic skills at a young age through their play. They learn how to run, jump, catch and throw in the course of their games, and it is fun. This is the start of gaining satisfaction from acquiring new skills. The fact that it is fun should be kept in mind, and that aspect is never lost in practising and developing new skills. In teaching youngsters, it is best to demonstrate and constructively guide them with minimal correction. They should be encouraged and only corrected occasionally when they aren't doing things properly. Greater success comes from constructive guidance without fault-finding and disapproval. Always keep in mind that most people thrive on positive reinforcement. They can take only a certain amount of criticism, and you may lose them altogether if you criticise them in a personal way.

Players like to try out various ways of performing the same activities. This exploratory play at practice should not be inhibited, at least in the early stages. This allows them to creatively learn the required skills and adjust their performance to their own individual capacities. Once a young tennis player had to use both hands to do a backhand. The coach was wise enough to allow the double backhand shot to continue and noticed how effective the youngster was at hitting the ball. That was the start of Bjorn Borg's tennis career. He won eleven Grand Slam titles. It should be fun. One way to teach long, accurate passing is to have one player run along the halfway line and throw the ball to two other players flanking him on the ten-metre line. It is initially difficult, but the 'game' can be set up in such a way that you will find they will be practising it in their own time.

The focus of attention for young rugby players needs to be on understanding the framework of the game and practising the whole skill. They do not have the basic skills needed to benefit from analysis and part drills. As they get older they can practice and refine specific skills more effectively, because they know how the part should fit in with the whole. Exercises can be invented with players running around cones, passing the ball or switching the ball to one another in drills designed to teach skills. This was the innovation that Alex Wyllie introduced to rugby. For younger age groups, the length and intensity of practice needs to be gauged carefully. Although pre-adolescents seem to recover faster after strenuous exercise, they do not tolerate as much work per practice. The amount they can tolerate increases with their physical maturity. They learn to endure longer practices, perform better and achieve a higher standard. Yet even the professional players seem to do better during the season if they can intersperse a day or two of rest with training regimes. I have seen situations where players come off the training field exhausted, yet after a Saturday game haven't expended half of their energy.

Practising and maintaining skills

Maintaining a high level of sporting skill does require constant practice. It is not sufficient to think that once a skill has been mastered there is little need for practice. It is necessary to constantly practise to maintain skills. Part of the reason is the need to set reinforcing pathways in the brain to trigger the appropriate responses. Players need to focus on cues that guide them as to what to do in particular situations. One example is practising when to time a pass so that the opponent is drawn to the ball carrier. This means not passing too early or too late. Most players learning this skill invariably pass too late and get caught, or do not put their outside support into the gap. To learn this skill, which is fundamental to rugby, requires focusing on cues regarding the alignment of defending players and when to pass the ball. It requires peripheral vision and a lot of experience in different situations. This is when teamwork becomes so important. It is demonstrated in the teamwork developed between Tana Umaga and Christian Cullen in the Hurricanes when they were timing their passes superbly to get each other into the gap at speed. Continuous practice is needed to maintain and fine-tune these skills.

One of the problems of teaching advanced performers is getting them to adapt to varying situations. Christian Cullen, when first in the All Blacks, was too keen to run in situations where kicking was probably the better option. In training it is important for players to experience these different situations and learn to make the right decision without losing their sense of adventure and spontaneity. Situations on the rugby field are rarely identical so players must learn a great variety of responses. Players must also learn to adjust to events as they change during the course of a game. This is where experience is so valuable. Giving players varied situations in which to practise accelerates their learning. This could include learning to take a high ball with players actually contesting it so that the conditions are similar to those in a game. There is also the need to train in different weather conditions. Players need to understand how to play in wet and slippery conditions. For example, few players realise that diving on the ball short of the line and being carried over in the slide is a great way to score a try. They need to practise how far they can skid along the ground. There is a need to learn to adjust to the opposition team's style of play by having squad members imitate the opponents during practice. You could try dealing with a flat defence, learning to counter the rolling maul or countering the wipers kick.

Practice in itself is not necessarily a guarantee that skills will improve. This issue is more obvious when one tries to learn to hit a golf ball. If the person's swing is defective, practice will only compound the problem. Some initial improvement may take place, but later development will be hindered because faulty techniques have been learned and become habitual. Such a case is hard to correct. Also, learning skills in a practice situation can be entirely different from applying those skills in a game. Take basketball, for example, where learning to dribble the ball is usually done bouncing the ball in front of the player, whereas in a game the player tends to shield the ball with his body.

Lack of improvement, or even deterioration in performance, can occur because of some unconscious faults that have crept into the way a skill is being executed. It can also indicate that a different method of training needs to be found. There may be a need to make significant changes to the way things that were previously successful are done. Even Tiger Woods had to reconstruct his golf swing. In making these changes, a player's performance can drop off until he or she learns to adjust to the new technique. This could relate to improved goal kicking techniques or changing the lines on which the backs run. It may take a while to master the new approach and players need to persist in spite of temporary setbacks.

At higher levels, where some unconscious errors may have crept into the way skills are executed, it is necessary to examine in detail the action sequences. Examples could include an extra and unnecessary step in trying to side-step, a variation in movement by the jumper in the lineout that gives away his intention to jump, or the backline positioning itself poorly in defence. These errors could creep in without the players being aware they are making such mistakes. In the case of side-stepping, the foot placement may be wasted by not stepping off sharply enough in the new direction.

The problem gets serious when errors creep in and are not rectified. To correct any problems, the coach must bring them to the players' attention so they know what changes are required, and then practise them so they become automatic responses in a game. Laurie Mains has a lot of expertise to guide players. Rod Macqueen's approach was to bring in specialists who could help to solve a problem. How you do it depends on your knowledge and operating style.

Problem solving and technical skills development

Effective problem solving is fundamental to the process of developing technical skills. Too often coaches deal with symptoms, rather than fixing the real problem. That is like fighting fire rather than dealing with the cause of the fire. The first thing to do is get a proper analysis of the situation. This means getting to the heart of the problem. It is asking questions like 'When is it happening?' and 'When is it not happening?' 'Who is involved and who isn't involved?' 'Where is it happening?' The approach requires a logical and deductive process, examining who is involved and in what situations the problem arises. Defining and analysing the problem and breaking it down into smaller parts is the key to getting it solved. It is then a matter of setting goals for improvement, looking at your options, deciding on the best solution and putting it into action. Underlying all this is cause-and-effect thinking and a willingness to receive feedback to see how the solution is working.

Developing and refining sporting skills is a process involving some trial and error. A good coach is able to break down the skill into components and get players to practice each component and then put it all together again. On television, we can watch players in certain positions and copy them. Someone like Grant Fox can explain skills such as goal kicking in great detail. He mastered the skill by concentrating on every minute aspect. Throwing the ball into lineouts can be learned by watching rugby games or even by watching basketball players shoot hoops. The standard of technical information on rugby available in New Zealand is vast. It is the premise of this book that too much emphasis is placed on technique without recognition of an overall learning and motivational context. At least we do have the technical knowledge.

Learning skills does involve practice and continuous revision to improve, along with the motivation to achieve mastery.

Mental practice

Mental practice between physical practices should be encouraged. There seems little doubt that mental practice can accelerate learning. An experiment was set up where one group of basketball players actually practised scoring hoops, another thought about all the actions required to make successful shots, and the last group was the control group and did nothing. The result showed there was little difference between the first two groups but the unprepared group did not score as well. This mental sequencing helps to set up the brain functions which facilitate the correct actions. Players practise the same move over and over again to reinforce the cortical path so reaction times are quicker.

Players can also think about scenarios that could happen on the field and how they would react to them. They might think about receiving the ball in a particular situation and how best to react under the given circumstances. It allows them to analyse their team's pattern and the way they play the game. There is now greater versatility of play in the roles of top players. Forwards now take up positions in the back line when the situation calls for it, and backs form the ruck when the play is beyond forward support. All this needs to be thought out.

Individual differences and personal motivation

Coaches need to identify the individual skills and attributes of each player and consider how they will best fit into the team. This can be part of selecting players for a particular team pattern. Most coaches do not have this luxury however, and need to build their team around the talent they have available. Each player brings some unique qualities to the position he or she holds. In other words, two players in the same position will perform in some way that is specific to the physical attributes and skills each has acquired. Michael Jones will have a different style of play from Josh Kronfeld in the same loose forward role. Identifying and developing these unique qualities is an important part of creating excellence in a team. This means getting to know players on an individual basis, discovering what motivates them and evaluating their particular attributes and how to develop these qualities within the framework of the team pattern.

Once a writer was trying to co-author a book with Vince Lombardi, the legendary American coach of the Green Bay Packers. They were getting nowhere because Lombardi was not a person who had a lot of anecdotes about sport. It wasn't his style. Just at the point where the writer was about to give up he decided to try one last technique using word association. He asked Lombardi to answer spontaneously what was in his mind each time he mentioned a word. He came out with a word and Lombardi spilled out a whole lot of information. Another word and the same thing. Thirty players' names later they had the book. Lombardi had a profound knowledge of each player, his skills, ability, motivation and, what was more important, how to make him a better sportsman. This was the secret of his success. Good coaches understand their players. They have insights into their strengths and weaknesses and the roles they play in the team. Knowing their concerns and aspirations helps the coach get the best out of them.

Organisation of practice

Effective coaching requires an environment that is conducive to training and assimilating skills. This starts with planning the practice and identifying the objectives you want to achieve. It requires a realistic assessment of what you can do in the time available. Writing down the programme and the time frames for each section gives focus to the practice. There needs to be a warm-up period, then skills training, physical fitness and running as a team. Having these activities properly allocated and knowing what you are trying to achieve means greater use is made of the time available and players see there is discipline and focus in the way the coach runs practice. The coach is acting as a role model by demonstrating his discipline and commitment to the team. Those who practise hard and are committed to the team are the ones who attain the highest standards of performance.

Adjust the overall plan as the practice progresses. There is a need for some flexibility. This can take into account the attitude of players, how they are working together and the performance standards they are reaching. The plan needs to have variety to create renewed interest. This could include introducing games or new exercises. Take care not to try to be too perfectionistic by insisting that drills must be perfect and not accepting anything less. Sometimes coaches over-emphasise the need for perfection. This is not to say that a coach should let the little things go. Right there is where the difference is made, according to Shula. He made his players do things until they got them right. However he would rather throw out a play or formation during practice than find out it could not be done correctly in the game.

Sound planning and organising is characteristic of top coaches. Sometimes coaches like Mains and Macqueen have been criticised for being over detailed and meticulous. Laurie Mains has been accused of spending hours preparing for meetings. John Wooden would spend an hour each morning just to plan that day's practice. He and his assistant coaches would evaluate what happened the day before, and then set down the practice schedule in fine detail – nothing was left to chance. Over the years Wooden became convinced that every detail was important and that success usually accompanied attention to detail. It was this, in his judgement, that made the difference between good teams and champion teams.

Participation and involvement

Giving the players a turn at coaching by having them conduct parts of the practice gives them responsibility and an opportunity for their ideas to be aired and tested. A very effective technique is to have the players develop their own moves. This gives ownership and a greater commitment to making them work. While it may lead to incorporating the odd dubious move that may not work, the involvement of the players and having them think things through more than compensates. I have seen moves that were flawed actually work because of the will of the players to make them happen. Once, after several attempts at a move, other team members said it should be dropped because it would never work. The initiator of the move maintained it could work and the next time it was called managed to score. The move wasn't a good one because too much time was spent feinting behind the advantage line before it was executed. The player had to battle through three lines of defenders to make the line. It was a bruising effort and as he limped back to the half way he was heard to say, 'I don't think we will try that one again!' It was just sheer determination to make it work that led to its success.

Skill development and feedback

Practice needs to reflect and reinforce achievement values. This means identifying the skills needed for each player and where their effort can make a difference. Techniques need to be learned and practised. But in learning a technique the most important thing for the player is to want to do it. This is the first lesson in tackling. is the player needs the determination to 'get them'. One of the most effective tackles I have ever seen was by a winger running across and doing a star jump that caught three forwards charging through together with the ball in hand. He just wanted to get them, and stopped a certain try.

In developing moves it is a matter of continuous improvement. Having goals like, 'We'll make this move work three times out of five', and then lifting the standard to 'four out of five' as players master the move, demonstrates effective goal setting and how to compare themselves against their own standards.

An important part of practice is providing feedback for players. Without feedback it isn't possible to learn how to improve. Imagine playing tenpin bowling if a curtain was pulled across the alley and you weren't able to see the pins. You wouldn't know if you had the right curve on the ball, or how you had scored. For your second shot you wouldn't know which pins were standing and where to aim. Too often feedback is negative, however. This needs to be balanced with positive feedback. Positive feedback would be to say that you knocked down eight pins, whereas negative feedback would say you missed two! On the surface there doesn't seem to be that much difference between the two types of feedback, but the first is more motivating.

Receiving feedback is one of the most important aspects of

learning and a valuable process in life. Giving and receiving feedback in an effective manner requires you to be open, honest and encouraging to players. Mains would always spell out the need for honesty in the relationship he had with his team. Most players want to be more effective, and providing them with feedback on their performance and progress is a powerful reward and intrinsic motivator. Phil Jackson feels that the relationship between a coach and his players is often fraught with tension because the coach is constantly critiquing each player's performance. The players need to understand that you are not attacking them personally when you correct mistakes.

Giving feedback has the greatest positive impact when a few simple guidelines are followed consistently. The message should be specific enough for the player to understand what he must do in order to gain greater task mastery. Beware of judgmental language, particularly words like 'stupid', 'sloppy' or other words that carry negative connotations. Also, monitor how much you are focusing on the exceptions in performance rather than recognising successful completion. In other words, reinforce and praise good performance. Skills build more effectively under positive reinforcement. Emphasise what is going right and more things start to go right.

Challenging and s-t-r-e-t-c-h-i-n-g players' abilities

Challenge needs to be continually presented to the players. Great teams are created from their ability to respond to challenge. This is an important ability that every player should possess. Earlier I talked about 'the hill' as a test of this ability to face a challenge. Now we must extend it to include other aspects of training and later match play. New moves must be rehearsed and improved upon. Mistakes will occur and encouragement must be given so players learn from what happened. There needs to be an urgency about getting things right. This means concentrating on improving skills like jumping higher in the lineout or executing a backline manoeuvre better. Perseverance is needed to maintain the concentration and effort. The underlying pursuit is excellence, continuously improving and getting more things right. It is a matter of learning how to be effective on the field. This doesn't involve trying to hit every ruck. It is better for a forward to hang back from a ruck where he can't be effective and be first to the next breakdown, than always arriving at the ruck after it has been formed. It is better to go at top pace when needed and half pace rather than three-quarter pace all game. Top pace is needed in order to be a try-scorer. This is an important lesson to learn. Early on in the season the scene should be set to stretch players' abilities and make improvements.

Attitude towards mistakes

When mistakes occur, take a positive approach. Don't stop players because they drop the ball. They need to play through the movement in order to learn from it. This means that they should recover the ball and get it under control. In a game the ball may get loose, so recovering it should be practised in training. It teaches players to pounce on the ball. Watch top players in action and it becomes clear that it is their ability to get to the ball and take action that separates them from the others. 'The ball, the ball, the ball,' is typically the cry of these players.

In today's rugby, the first to the ball usually wins possession. Incorporating this into training means building up fast reactions to the breakdown of play and changing attitudes to mistakes. What usually happens in practice is that when the ball is dropped the movement comes to a halt and players wait for the coach to say something before repeating the play. Often it is not the mistake that is the problem in a game, but the lack of recovery from a mistake. This is done poorly because players are hesitant when a mistake occurs. Phil Jackson needed to shout from the bench, 'Why are you looking at me, you already know you made a mistake.' Remember, we don't expect 'no mistake rugby' so there need to be strategies to deal with breakdowns.

Drills and games

Some competition can be fun at practice. It can include initiative exercises such as having teams of four or five competing to get their ball to the other end of the field first using any means they like. If they drop the ball they have to start from the beginning. This means they have to work out for themselves how to do it quickest. Kicking the ball to each other is possibly the fastest method but it has a high risk factor. The safest option is for one player to run the length of the field, but that is slow. There could be combinations involving kicking, passing and running. In the gymnasium initiative exercises can be staged by assigning chairs, a bench, rope and any other gear that may be on hand to the team and challenging them to get to the opposite wall without touching the floor. Using each item only once, they have to work out the best way. These types of games have been popular with business managers doing out-door training, and the army has used similar exercises to evaluate team initiative and leadership. They are fun to participate in and can be good a contrast to the drills that are a necessary part of practice. It stops practice from becoming boring if there is some variation.

It is not my intention in this book to outline many drills or games that can be used for developing skills. This area is well covered by other published material. Obvious things include: forward unit skills that involve running with the ball, short passing, continuity and support play. The mechanics of scrums and lineouts need to be sorted out, as well as technique variations in rucks and mauls. The backs need to sort out positioning, alignment and accurate passing. Once again, the mechanics of lines of running and how to create space need to be looked at. All the techniques need to be analysed and refined. A quick look at rugby coaching on the internet will provide references to this source of information. I will, however, outline some games and drills I have used to good effect.

Touch rugby when played properly teaches ball-handling skills, running and timing the pass. To make sure that it is played properly, I introduce the rule that it must be a two-handed touch. This draws the defender right onto the ball carrier. In another variation that also works well, the ball carrier is able to run through the first touch, but if he does so and is touched again possession goes to the other side. This game is played in a narrow area such as between the try-line and the twenty-two. This teaches players to break through the tackle, and how and when to unload. Players are not allowed to score if they have been touched once. Every now and then you can give some pointers on how they are playing, such as how well they are drawing their opposition before passing.

Practise gaining the initiative

Reinforcing the need to take the initiative should be another one of the focal points at practice. The coach should emphasise that the initiative is gained through speed, variation and taking the game to the opposition. Developing an offensive defence is a great way to gain the initiative. This approach seeks psychological ascendancy not only in attack but in every phase of the game. Quite a different mentality builds when players think they are attacking when the opposition has the ball. Their job is to drive them backwards and regain possession. An aggressive defence disrupts the opposition's pattern of play and gives you the initiative. It robs the opposition of imagination and the willingness to take chances. Emphasise the fact that a player is as much a hero for saving a try as he is for making one. A whole new mentality can be developed in the team regarding defence.

Having possession is the best way to maintain the initiative, as the team is more able to dictate play. Variation is a key to keeping the initiative when in possession. It forces the opposition to hesitate and wait to see what is going to happen before they react, and these vital moments give the edge to the offensive side. It forces them into reacting rather than being pro-active. At practice it is therefore essential that the team is able to vary play. When running the team through a simulated game, insist that they do not repeat the same play. They should keep introducing variations, not only from set play, but also in the second phases as well, and even when there is a breakdown. By doing this they learn to work impromptu moves and it stretches their imagination. Gradually a whole set of plays begin to emerge which find spontaneous expression in a match. Once coach Wooden was told by his basketball players that they were up against a team that was so well drilled they were perfect. His response was to say, 'Great, we will know exactly what the play is and where the ball will be and so we will know how to counter it. That is a lot easier than when play breaks down and they try something spontaneous!'

Points, points and more points

Besides instilling the need for the initiative, the other fundamental to highlight is the focus on points, points and more points. At practice, have players think about this all the time. It can easily be demonstrated that most do not think this way. I start the first training session by instructing the team to simulate a real game. When they pass the ball along the back line, I yell 'down' and they put the ball on the ground, the forwards go over the top and ruck it back and the pattern repeats itself until they run out of room on the field. Once again I start them off at about the half way line and the same thing is repeated. During this time I keep asking them 'What are the three P's of rugby?' They often come up with position, possession and pace – or some other variation. Usually their enthusiasm for having me as a guest coach is waning by the fourth or fifth time we do the same drill.

I keep asking, 'What are the fundamentals of this game?' At some stage a player will finally force the ball over the try-line. Finally it has happened! Up until then they have being forming rucks and mauls, getting the ball back when they were just short of the line. It is points, points and more points they really want. The game is about scoring points. This isn't consciously in the minds of most players. When a break happens in a game, they are usually just pleased that they are getting up the field! In their minds, they play the game between the two try-lines and give no thought to scoring. Ask anyone the length of a rugby field and they won't include the deadball area. As a coach you can stand over the line and point out in a dramatic way that that is where the game is decided. It is the responsibility of everyone to score tries. Go back to the half way, this time with the three P's in mind. The players become totally focused on getting over that line. With a bit of stoking up, I have seen players so determined to score that they have run the last twenty metres head down and launched themselves at the line, ignoring my calls of, 'Down! down! down!' They had developed a lust for the line. Top players invariably have this built into them. They have learnt that the game is about scoring tries. I call those ten metres in front of the try line 'The Zone of Opportunity.' It is where the try-scorers make the difference.

Most practices do not have a focus on the try-line. It takes only twenty seconds to score a try from anywhere on the field. Three or four tries are possible in every game. It is the teamwork, the initiative and the focus on the line that will make it happen. During practice the support players call, 'Go, go, go,' leaving the ball carrier in no doubt about what he should do. If they want the ball because they are in a better position, they call the player by name. Players need to be try hungry. Most are line-shy. When a break occurs, they should be sprinting to get in the play. With variation, offensive play and a focus on scoring tries, the mentality in the team changes dramatically. It leads to try scoring.

Patterns of play

The overall objective of practice is to develop a pattern of play that the team is going to use. While some adjustment is made to tactics when playing any given opposition, a team mainly develops its own pattern. Player skills, and the best way for the team to gain the initiative and score tries should underlie the formation of this pattern. It is usually an evolutionary process. Players need to understand the underlying pattern as it develops. At practice, the team needs to run through the pattern and its variations repeatedly. Being able to simulate the conditions experienced in a match as closely as possible helps to accelerate learning.

A basic pattern is to ensure that the ball gets in front of the forwards. By having them run forward they create the conditions that allow them to smash through the opposition's defence. In terms of back play, I have always preferred a flat formation, with plenty of moves worked off the players. This is a style that Bob Dwyer's World Champion team developed. Emphasis is placed on running straight at the defence to put them under pressure. The variation in moves creates uncertainty in the opposition. The attacking team has the advantage of being able to inject the fullback or winger into the backline to create the extra man in order to penetrate the defence, or provide an overlap. The opposition cannot easily respond to this, as they do not know where the attacking team is going to direct its attack and have to keep all parts of the field covered. The key is to draw the defenders by straight running. Passing without drawing a defender means that a drifting defence nullifies the move. The biggest mistake a player can make is to run to avoid the defence. This draws the tacklers onto the teammate running alongside, to whom he is going to pass the ball. This is more likely to happen when the backline stands in depth. Very precise angles and moves need to be developed to play the flat backline pattern. Practising this formation and the detail of the moves under pressure is what is needed. This can be simulated during practice. Players need to learn to stay tight and not to drift in order to ensure that the extra player is brought into the gap.

'It almost goes without saying that tactics are the soul of rugby. Nothing in the world pays a team so well as accurate performance of sound and sensible tactics.'[4] These are the words of Billy Stead, the 1905 vice-captain and later captain of the All Blacks. In his book written in 1906 he outlined the success of the All Black 'Originals' as coming from having innovative ideas and superior tactics. He believed that superior tactics would overcome a stronger opposition. His tactics were based around moves. Every player gave the closest attention to studying and understanding these tactics. These moves did not have to be complicated, in fact he thought the simpler the better. 'Though simpler the better, it was not a case of the fewer the better.'[5] He believed that the greater the variety of moves that a side possessed, the greater their chances of springing surprises on the opposition. It may play one set of moves on one day and another on the next, and it may reserve a few particular moves for very occasional use. He believed that such a side would be a constant embarrassment to all others it met. In his introduction to his book he quoted Napoleon's advice to those who would study the art of war, which said that one should read the history of the great campaigns of the great generals of the past. One year I noted down the moves in the Super Twelve and NPC which resulted in tries. While I didn't see that many games, I ended up with a notebook full of moves. And these were only the ones that resulted in tries! Perhaps there are lessons we can learn from the 'Originals.'

Players should be instructed where to run on defence. For example, the loose forwards and the number eight should have a clear idea of defending from a scrum. The back line needs to know whether they are using man-on-man defence, a drifting defence or a defence that hangs back in depth. To maintain the initiative I recommend a mixture of these strategies. Nearer the opposition's line, I advocate a man-on-man offensive approach as it puts pressure on them. A drifting defence counters the opposition's outside backs. In-depth defence works well on a wet day. With bigger squads at the professional level, it is easy to organise simulated situations at practice as they often have the equivalent of two teams. With fewer reserves it can still be simulated. The role of the 'opposition' is to help the team learn offensive and defensive patterns. Sometimes they get too competitive and are inclined to disrupt the practice. It needs to be explained to them that they are contributing by helping the others to learn and they are part of the coaching team for the exercise.

The types of play that can be practised using touch rugby are team patterns like back line moves, how to deal with a flat defence, and counter attack. When players are touched in the act of passing the ball the play can continue just as it would in a game if they were passing as they were tackled. Such simulations can teach quite sophisticated patterns of play. At other times, the team can be run as if they were in a game. The more the players can imagine the 'real' opposition, the better the learning process. They imagine various situations and how they would play them. This pre-conditions them to interpret situations when they arise and they are more likely to respond appropriately during an actual game.

All these exercises are also building teamwork. Rugby is a game that relies heavily on teamwork. There is a higher rate of inter-dependency among the team members than in any other sport. The complexity of the game means time and effort need to be put into moulding the team and its pattern. Teamwork can overcome superior opposition. One of the great things about rugby is that superior teamwork, motivation and tactics can overcome better individual talent in an opposition team. This is why John Wooden concentrated on his own team and rarely concerned himself about the opposition. He believed in his team playing their own game, and that quality would win out in the end. At practice, reinforce the importance of the team playing its game. This is the way they will stamp their initiative on the game.

Physical and mental balance

When I watch professional teams practise I often see a lot of physical conditioning and contact taking place. Often tackle bags or padded shields are used, or the 'opposition' is in protective gear, but there seems to be too much emphasis on this physical conditioning. Too much conditioning can rob players of some of the enthusiasm needed to play the game, and tends to produce a Spartan type of warrior. The Spartans lived in southern Greece and were noted for their physical courage. Children were reared in a semi-military way, and in adolescence and adulthood spent endless hours rehearsing the drills necessary for war. They even learned to speak in short concise sentences in everyday conversation as preparation for quick communication on the battlefield.

In contrast, the Athenians in the city-state to the north were more balanced in the way they developed their people. It was their passion, planning and skill that led to the defeat of the Persians in the battle at Marathon. Victory led to the rise of Greek civilisation and a culture that has heavily influenced Western civilisation. To Plato, the Greek philosopher, education was a balance of mind and body. The modern professional player can end up like a Spartan, physically conditioned but lacking as a person. I have seen school teams drilled along Spartan or All Black lines and, while they were formidable, they lacked the zest for the game. They became more mechanical. Thinking and passion is still a big part of the game. To some extent this is getting drilled out of our professional players because of emphasis on the physical conditioning that is required, and the extended season they play.

There is a need for physical conditioning but a team is at its best when it taps the thinking and inner spirit of players so they develop determination and passion for the game. Ian Foster, who coached

Waikato to the NPC finals, believes that physical conditioning can be overdone at the top level. I am against being too physical at practice, particularly for the younger grades. I have seen it work as a one-off exercise. Tackling teammates cannot be done with the same determination as in an actual game. During practice it is inclined to teach players to scrag each other rather than tackle. Getting the balance right is one of the intricate tasks of the coach. At the start of the season it is necessary to focus more on the toughening-up process, and as the season progresses the players will become more conditioned from playing the game.

All Blacks build up to the World Cup

An outstanding example of preparation was the way Laurie Mains prepared the All Blacks for the World Cup. He organised training camps and in his book *Laurie Mains*, by Bob Howitt and Robin McConnell, he outlined how he approached each camp. The overall theme of the first camp was team building and fitness. The second camp concentrated on fitness and skills development. Physical fitness assessments were made and individual targets were moved to higher levels of attainment.

The second camp also dealt with basic tactics. This involved such things as the back three (the fullback and two wingers) dealing with high kicks. He felt this was particularly pertinent because they had conceded some costly tries in the previous two years by allowing opponents to beat them to the punch when chasing 'bombs.' The first skill to master was catching the ball under pressure. Next came the subtle art of protecting the catcher without resorting to blatant obstruction. He showed the support players how to position themselves in a direct line with the person catching the ball. They couldn't stick out their elbows or physically impede oncoming opposition players, but they were entitled to run directly back toward the person waiting for the ball. And he pointed out that they were legally able to stand in front of the player as he took the ball. So they practised that a lot.

He wanted to impress on players that they needed to accept that they had to make improvements in individual skills in order to play the sort of game they were aiming to achieve. He placed considerable emphasis on sprinting. Not the basic 100-metre goal-post to goal-post dash that players have traditionally indulged in, but about the technique and structure of sprinting. His theory was that if, with the high-speed type of game they planned, they could improve everyone's sprinting technique, backs and forwards, the whole team was going to benefit.

Interestingly, at the conclusion of this camp Mike Brewer was disappointed because Mains hadn't trained the players hard, hadn't run them into the ground. So Mains explained to him, in the presence of the whole squad, the reason why. At that stage of the team's aerobic development programme, running the guts out of them wasn't going to achieve anything. It would have been disruptive and contrary to the gradual build-up he was working on. Besides, it was not the purpose of this camp, which took place before Christmas.

At the third camp in February, Mains introduced saturation coaching with an emphasis on the drills and basic techniques that would be required to play the pattern he wanted. He wanted to put the players through the physical demands that would allow him to assess their courage, will, and fortitude. This camp would show which players had qualities that would surface at crucial times and allow the team to win test matches. A lot of time was spent on creating tackle situations and how to clear the ball without breaking the law, because this was an area in which the All Blacks teams traditionally had conceded lots of penalties. The ball coming out after tackles was too slow, so they worked at getting faster ball without giving away penalties. The aim was to have the forwards so conversant with each match situation that they would act instinctively to do the right thing. He kept the forwards at it for hours on end, until they had the right feel.

The other skill Mains really wanted to foster was long, accurate passing by the backs – passing that skipped one or two players and covered long distances with speed and accuracy. Also, the backs had to be able to decide whether to punch through a tackle or, knowing they were going to be tackled, learn how to confront their opponent. Mains maintained there was a difference. If they knew they were going to be tackled, their first priority was to set up quality ball for their support players. They had to develop a technique that would allow the ball to be cleared quickly.

Mains found the mental attitude coming out of this camp something he had never experienced before. The team sensed that they were creating an edge. They believed that no other nation would be putting anything like this amount of time and effort into preparation. It wasn't just the physical exertion but the manner in which they were perfecting basic skills that was making the difference.

The fourth camp a few weeks later set out to create the conditions of camp three. This time a major focus was on influencing the opposition's defensive patterns as it was important to stop them drifting across the field. They could be held straight by the manner in which the All Blacks aligned their own back line. The alignment of the back line was so important that Mains would not let the forwards release the ball to the halfback until they had their alignment and width right. Then he had an exercise called 'Ten Times Through'. The players were required to execute a different move each time the ball went through the back line, whether it was a simple miss pass, a double miss, a cut or a dummy cut. All this worked up so it was done under extreme physical pressure, so they could to do such things on match day. They practised these tactics until the players did them almost automatically, even though most of them could hardly run any more.

The other emphasis was on their own defence. Mains found it useful working with two squads, as one would could practise defence while the other team had a crack at attack. The intensity rose during some sessions, and Mains felt it became extremely competitive – to the point of being over competitive. He was always careful to keep control of the situation. Lifting it to this final intensity allowed the players to perfect the precision in their techniques. (The information on the Mains' training camps has been taken with permission from the book *Laurie Mains*, by Bob Howitt and Robin McConnell.)

This explanation of Mains' programme in developing the All Blacks highlights the points made in this chapter about training. He managed to bring it all together and one can understand his disappointment at the food poisoning that robbed them of the opportunity to play their best in the final.

Summary

This chapter highlights the motivational context for conducting team practices and for players learning new skills. Practice sessions have to be tied to the values associated with high achievement thinking and the approach I advocate for the game. They need to cover physical and mental conditioning as well as skills and team patterns of play. The emphasis should be on developing players who can think for themselves and learn from their experiences and the training they receive. It has not been the purpose of this chapter to go into the intricacies of all the techniques and skills required for each position. This information is readily available through other sources.

---

1. Ray Didinger (ed.), *Game Plans For Success*
2. Wayne Bennett, *Don't Die With The Music In You*
3. Joseph Romanos, *Great NZ Coaches*
4. D Gallaher and W J Stead, *The Complete Rugby Footballer*
5. D Gallaher and W J Stead, *The Complete Rugby Footballer*

Chapter 8

TEAM SPIRIT

Team spirit refers to the players' collective attitude, and developing this spirit is an essential aspect of coaching. The coach helps to bring the team together by emphasising commitment to each other and promoting the ideals of teamwork. Team spirit is characterised by a positive attitude and willingness to co-operate as part of a team. Members should hold each other in high regard and focus on the task in hand. The coach inculcates such attitudes in the team. They are seen in the selfless way players contribute to their team and respond to the call for excellence. It is about commitment to others and the team effort. It is the spirit, the will to win, and the will to excel that creates the enduring quality in a team and makes them stand out as a group that possesses something special.

Team spirit is not directly related to skill or ability. The difference between players with good team spirit and those without it is a sense of purpose and will power. It is the culmination of belief and commitment that is so intense and palpable that it is readily recognisable in the way members interact and behave. It is about creating a team culture, shared values and beliefs that exist in the team. Values are what are important to team members, and beliefs include how things should be done. They are manifest during team talks, in the changing room and the on the field. This spirit is all-encompassing.

Creating this unity takes time and requires continuous effort. It starts at the very first practice and is repeatedly reinforced by selecting players who build team spirit, encouraging them to be committed to one another and reinforcing their contribution to the team. This means that the best player doesn't automatically get selected. I would rather have a player who plays to the fullest of his ability and contributes to the team effort than one who may be individually more skilled but is not contributing to the team. This doesn't mean that you select only players who get along together. That would form social cliques that could destroy team cohesion. It is how individuals contribute to the overall performance of the team that counts. This depends on more than just their playing ability, but it is not based on whether you like or dislike them.

Nothing can stop a team with the right mental attitude from achieving its goal, and nothing can help a team with the wrong mental attitude. Weakness of attitude becomes weakness of character in the team. In order to be successful, attitude is equally as important as ability. It is the attitude in the team, the spirit of the players, that will determine the outcome more than anything else. Players who are committed to each other will work together to win. A little difference in attitude and team spirit makes a big difference on the sports field. The root of true achievement lies in the will to become the best that a team can become. This can only be achieved through dedication, trial and overcoming setbacks. It is an indomitable spirit that is about getting back up after being knocked down.

Top coaches' commitment to team spirit

To Lombardi team spirit was first and foremost individual commitment to the team. To him the price of success was hard work, dedication to the job at hand, and, win or lose, the determination to apply themselves to the best of their ability. He built in the team a feeling of oneness, of dependence on one another and of strength derived from unity. To him there was only one way to succeed in anything, and that was to give it everything. That is what he demanded of himself and his players. He made them realise that if the mind is willing, the body will follow. He showed players that by working hard and using their minds, they could overcome their weaknesses to the point where they could be the best. The qualities he encouraged were sacrifice and self-denial. These were combined with a disciplined will that refused to give in. He believed it was a state of mind which he called 'character in action.' His team, the Green Bay Packers, never lost a game. They just ran out of time.

Essentially, Lombardi believed that battles were primarily won through team spirit. To him that was what it was all about. His players didn't play for individual glory. They did it because they were committed to one another. Team spirit meant believing in themselves and having the courage, the determination, the dedication, the competitive drive and the willingness to make sacrifices for the things that were worthwhile. It was not that 'winning was everything – but the will to win is everything.' To achieve this he would gather his players around him. He laughed, he cried, he motivated them to do almost anything. He communicated with human emotions. To him, leadership was the power to inspire. His enthusiasm, his spirit, was infectious. To him, teams didn't go physically flat, they went mentally stale. Yet we see newspaper reports equating players' performances to the form of racehorses rather than evaluating their mental states.

Lombardi was a member of the 'old school' of coaching. He was more of an authoritarian and disciplinarian than would be accepted today. But he had also grasped the concepts of human motivation. He believed in mental toughness, which included the qualities of sacrifice, self-denial, dedication, fearlessness, and loyalty. He believed that games were won in the hearts of men. Players responded to leadership in a most remarkable way. This leadership was based on the power to inspire. There are average coaches who just have knowledge, and then there are good coaches who have knowledge and can get it across. Top coaches not only can get the knowledge across but can also fire up a team to play above their level.

Don Shula is a modern football coach who espoused the same values. Players picked for the Miami Dolphins already had skills and talent. Shula saw his job as instructing, disciplining and inspiring them to do better than they thought they could. To him, winning and losing didn't depend on trick plays or using new strategies each week. It came down to a matter of motivating players to work hard and be prepared to play as a team. To him that was what really counted. In other words, he was coaching them. He often asked himself what made a great coach? He believed it was passion and enthusiasm that created a burning in the gut, the desire to win that won't quit.

Shula was a coach who let his adrenalin flow and his emotions out in order to inspire his players. He wanted the relationship with his team to be one of mutual respect. 'I want my players to respect me for giving them everything that I have to prepare them to play the best they can play.' His respect for them came from knowing that the players were willing to give him all that they had to prepare themselves to be ready to play. To gain credibility the coach must have trust. It is not a naive trust, but it is not possible to develop team spirit if the coach is continually suspicious and defensive. There is a need to be up front with players. It is a matter of being honest and direct with them and admitting mistakes when they occur. These attitudes possessed by Shula came across to the team. To maintain team spirit, he believed that when a team wins the coach cannot afford too be arrogant or over confident, and if they lose the coach cannot engage in blame.

Notre Dame's Lou Holtz believed that effective coaches could help teams short on talent win famous victories simply by preparing them physically and making sure they are focused and prepared to make the sacrifices necessary to raise their play to another level. How well they did was determined by their attitude. He exalted them to be committed to excellence, to do everything to the best of their ability. To achieve this it was necessary to continually encourage players. This meant teaching them not to be afraid of failure. To Holtz there was no such thing. Win or lose, if they believed in their hearts that they had done their best, they could live with the result. He couldn't stomach mediocrity. Winning was about focusing on what the team had instead of what they lacked. He was always amused and saddened to see the turmoil players put themselves through by comparing themselves to others. To him this was playing useless mind games. He thought competition was about welcoming adversity as a test of resolve. It wasn't about inflated ability or creating false confidence by hyping players up. Rather, winning was about setting standards that were a real measure of their dedication. It was being willing to give everything they had. It was a matter of self-respect – never accepting anything less than their best effort.

Team cohesion is also built through traditions and expectations. The culture needs to be formed around the belief in teamwork. Laurie Mains and Rod Macqueen placed particular focus on this aspect of team development. Macqueen totally changed the way Australian teams prepared by taking them away to a resort in the north where they could be together in a relaxed and informal environment. Previously they had been centred in a city hotel with practice fields across town. In the new setup, players shared condominiums together and practice facilities were close at hand. It all went towards creating a family atmosphere, which built a culture of commitment to the team.

Rod Macqueen believed that success on the field would only come if player bonding and team spirit were continually boosted. He also recognised the need for a players' committee to assist in the organisation of social activities. When forming the new Brumbies team with players from the other states, he promised that he would create an atmosphere that would allow individuals to come together as a team. What was also important was that players should have the right attitude and necessary commitment to the team. He wanted to instil the same team spirit in the Wallabies when he took on the national coaching role. He didn't subscribe to aggressive psyching up tactics where the coach ranted and raved. This type of passion was an excuse for those who hadn't done their preparation. He saw passion in quite a different way. Passion to Macqueen was something that needed to be built over a long period.

Leadership strategies and team spirit

Team spirit comes from inculcating attitudes in the team that are about serving one another. It starts with beliefs about team building. It it important to understand how players contribute to the team as well as knowing their sporting ability. I once had to award 'player of the day'. I gave it to the emergency person who had enthusiastically supported the team from the sideline and didn't even get onto the field. The other players thought it was great, as he was as much part of the team as they were.

Teams do take on the personality of the coach. In studies I have done I have come to the conclusion that the greatest influence on team spirit is the style of leadership. The values of the coach are translated to the team. John Adshead personified enthusiasm and achievement values in his epic journey with the New Zealand All Whites soccer team to the World Cup in Spain. He could watch his team playing, chew gum and make achievement statements to a television crew all at the same time!

One of the most important tasks is to encourage members of the team to give themselves wholeheartedly to the team effort. This has to be exemplified in the approach of the coach. When the players move from 'me' to 'we', then they are starting to think as a team and a powerful new consciousness emerges that is greater than the sum of their individual efforts. They must see that the coach wants the best for them, and while he is sometimes tough and demanding he is always there helping them to improve.

The relationship between the coach and players is not a matter of popularity. If a coach wants to be liked he won't want to make hard decisions and, in the end, players will lose respect. The only way to get respect is to earn it. Players should come to realise that the coach is not motivated by his ego but by a desire for them to do well. Without this respect, little can be achieved. It is not a matter of saying what players want to hear but of doing the right things. It is about leadership. The fact that the coach is asking players to push themselves beyond their limits will automatically mean that he won't always be popular. If the coach is concerned with being liked then it will be hard to get the players to push their limits.

Moulding team spirit takes on many facets. First, the intention of the coach must be made perfectly clear. How he views teamwork and the commitment of players to one another is a primary mover in the attitudes the team will develop. This team spirit needs to be reinforced. It parallels the Christian message of commitment to others. The feelings that are engendered in a team that has come together with a powerful team spirit are spiritual in nature. It is about giving of one's self for the good of the team. This is a powerful motivator because it calls on the desire we all have to be close to one another. For some it may be something that has to be learned. It is an opportunity to get in touch with a manly spirit that binds a group together in a powerful way. Such comradeship develops an intense desire within the team to do its best.

Leadership strategies come to the fore in developing team spirit. These were covered in Chapter Four. Communicating the philosophy about teamwork is the start (envisioning). The coach needs to outline what the important attitudes, beliefs and values in the team are, and what is expected of each player. It is possible to inculcate achievement values into the team by this process. This is about reinforcing values such as courage, committment and fortitude. It shouldn't be handed down as the Ten Commandments. Macqueen got his teams to establish their own standards and to help reinforce them. This is what building a team culture is about. It's the norm that governs how players approach the way they train and interact with each other. It identifies what is important and what the explicit and implicit rules are. Values are a far more powerful way of reinforcing behaviours than rules. The coach needs to exemplify these values in practical ways (be the role model).

There is a place for rules but these should be kept to a minimum. By not imposing too many rules, the coach builds up an attitude toward commonly held beliefs and values that reinforce commitment to the team. Some coaches feel threatened when players start exerting their independence. They try to keep a tight reign on their behaviour by insisting on rules and routines that establish the conformity they want. Today's players want to be involved in the decisions about how they play the game and the development of strategies (stimulating thinking).

Players need to have things carefully explained to them about team spirit (mentoring). This should explain about how things are done inside the team. It helps them to reflect on how they can contribute. This is part of transformational leadership, converting players into a tightly bonded team. Stories about previous members can highlight the values that have been handed down (referring). Before a test match, Macqueen would have one of the former Wallabies address the team, and it proved to be a very empowering experience. Players reported how enthralled they were by the stories of those who had gone before them. These stories carry important messages and values that help to carry on the traditions and spirit of a team. It is exactly the same when players represent the traditions of their school or club.

The coach reinforces the message of team spirit by the way he keeps in touch with players at an individual level as well as the way he relates to the team. Showing interest and concern for players demonstrates commitment to their development. Noticing their effort and contribution to the team helps to direct the attention of players toward goals, standards and preferred ways of doing things (monitoring). Communicating positive evaluations of how players are contributing to the team reinforces the values of team spirit. Rewards for contributing to the team increase their commitment (reinforcing). Such rewards can include lifting the players' image in the team, extending opportunities to that player and celebrating their success. Conversely there need to be sanctions against inappropriate behaviour by players. These may include things such as excluding offenders from the team, reducing time with them or penalising them for operating outside accepted standards.

A coach needs to have the ability to encourage players to improve. This means he or she must have a positive regard for what players can achieve and recognise the value of positive feedback. Taking such notice means the coach is able to give genuine recognition and praise when players are progressing. It also allows the coach to correct any deviations from the accepted ways of doing things (providing feedback). Such coaches gain satisfaction from seeing players fulfil their potential by providing support and inspiring self-improvement. Not only do they build an attitude of self-improvement in players but also a strong sense of self-esteem. Such coaches actively involve team members in planning, goal setting and decisions where appropriate. Their focus is on helping team members to discover their own strengths and capabilities, often by getting players to think for themselves about how to improve their performance. Emphasis is placed on understanding players and showing enthusiasm when instructing and coaching them. In return, such coaches gain respect, and players know they can rely on them for support and encouragement. The Warrior's Stacey Jones, when asked what made the difference in the team's performance in 2002, attributed it to Coach Daniel Anderson's ability to make them believe in themselves. In other words, he developed the self-esteem of players.

The coach needs to influence how the team moulds together. This is a reciprocal relationship (influencing). Team spirit is built through co-operation and treating each other with respect. It can be difficult for the coach, who must push players to perform better on the one hand, and on the other try to develop a relationship that is supportive. This is where respect is paramount. Players need to feel they can influence the coach. This is more likely if participative methods are used so decisions are fully understood and accepted.

Creating the right setting requires pulling together shared values, beliefs and expectations that endorse an achievement-oriented team spirit. It means helping players have an enriched experience in the way they relate to others in the team. They should share a spirit that helps to reinforce their determination to do well. Such an environment allows them to grow and develop as players. They become more resourceful and confident in their ability to make a difference to the outcome of the game. To be in a team where the beliefs and actions of its members provide a unique team spirit is enormously uplifting and motivating. The setting that develops team spirit is created by the ideas, assumptions, expectations and traditions of a high-achieving and committed group.

These recommendations for team building evolved from the leadership strategies outlined earlier. These strategies have mobilised team members not only to give their best effort on the field, but also to contribute as members of the team off the field as well. They enable players to use their own initiative and experience, rather than limiting or constraining their actions. Players are able to contribute within the guidelines that have been set. This is what leadership strategies are about. They form the process by which the coach sets the purpose or direction for individual players and the team, and gets them to move in that direction with full commitment. Team spirit is essentially an attitude of mind. It is more than a verbal commitment. It generates the will to struggle for shared aspirations. This is how leadership is defined. It enhances players' performance and makes them feel empowered to give their best. The springboard is team spirit.

Reinforcing team spirit

Symbols and rituals are powerful ways of reinforcing values associated with team spirit. Rituals such as team huddles bring members together into a tightly bound group that symbolises their unity. Having a dress code with jerseys, club ties and jackets gives identity as a group. Often the power and influence of these symbols and rituals are overlooked. The pre-match build-up is a ritual. Respect for the team colours needs to be a given. Players should not practice in the team's jersey. It is special and should only be used in a match. They will learn to honour the jersey. It represents the passion for excellence and needs to be worn proudly. It is the same regardless of whether you are representing a school, a club or your country.

To develop team spirit, it is necessary to take time with players and express a genuine interest in them. The coach must listen, ask questions and accept the players for who they are. Such coaches are open about their thoughts and feelings and encourage a reciprocal response. They are willing to give more of themselves when helping players. This positive regard for players leads to improved team relationships. Teambuilding means creating an atmosphere of co-operation and friendship among players so they enjoy being part of the team. Players can have nicknames within the team. Often they arise from incidents within the team. This helps to build an in-group language which reinforces the identity of the team.

Social functions provide an opportunity to meet in a non-sports environment. Many people join teams for the camaraderie and the friendships that are built through playing a sport. Some teams can become like family. Involvement of parents in junior teams and partners in senior teams makes a difference. Team camps give players the opportunity to get to know each other in more depth. This bonding produces a shift in thinking that makes commitment to the group paramount.

Sir Peter Blake regularly used inspirational speeches to renew and focus the efforts of team members. Their very name states the basic value around which the group came together – Team New Zealand. It is not always easy to hold a strong-minded group together. Personalities and differing values test the resolve of a team to stay together. There is a constant strain between encouraging members to work to their full potential – resulting in high levels of motivation and teamwork – and putting their own interests before that of the team. There is a need for balance. Players do look to advance their own success, and need to do this in conjunction with the team's success. Personal responsibility is the formula that underlies getting this balance. This is how the individual's contribution creates synergy for the team. The coach needs to encourage honest commitment and have expectations about being enthusiastic, co-operative and supportive of others in the team.

As team spirit develops, it is important that cliques do not build up. This might happen among the older players or some particular sub-group in the team. Of course, selection should be based on a player's ability to contribute to the team and not on whether you like him personally. Cliques in teams can make life difficult for a coach. Togetherness is an important quality in the team. It does not mean that the team has to spend all their time together or socialise with each other all the time. It does mean that when they are together there are no divisions in the team.

There was a legacy in the All Blacks that the senior players had more privilege. In Colin Mead's day, the back of the bus was reserved for those who had been in the team for some time. Graham Mourie heralded a change – all members were considered equal regardless of whether they were new to the team or long serving. Perhaps Michael Jones epitomised this approach. Many younger players have recounted how this legend of a footballer approached them at their first rep practice and made them feel welcome.

New players or those with a different background need to be accepted. Once Vince Lombardi was with his team in the Deep South when racial segregation was still practised and was politely informed that a black player would have to come through the back door to the restaurant. He accepted that– so the whole team came through the back door. Lombardi would not stand for cliques or special privileges for some players. It runs counter to the attitudes necessary for building team spirit.

Team spirit goes beyond the need for task accomplishment. Superior skill and ability are not the only requirements of a successful team. Sport is a fast-paced and aggressive environment that can cause participants to be hard driving. Success can lead to a downfall when over-confidence is bred from such behaviour. This is a dilemma because aggressive and competitive behaviour can help individuals to do well on an individual basis. The coach must keep firmly in the minds of players that when the team wins everyone wins.

There is always the need to keep re-establishing a feeling of unity among players. Everyone needs to show a balanced concern for the task at hand and the needs of team members. Reminding players of the 'big picture' helps to keep them focused. The New Zealand Warriors rugby league team has regularly become over-confident after a big win and then lost to a weak side in the following game. They would get carried away with their own importance. Under their new coach, Daniel Anderson, there has certainly been a change to a more achievement-oriented approach.

In contrast to ego and self-interest is trust, which is the emotional glue that holds every team together. It transforms a group of committed individuals into a team of individuals committed to each other. The essence of team spirit means that each member shares a common ideal and embraces a common goal. Regardless of their differences, they strive shoulder to shoulder, confident in one another's faith, trust, and commitment.

In the end, team spirit can be summed up in five short words quoted by basketball player Michael Jordan, 'We believe in each other.' Unity and resolve are the greatest strengths in a team. They form the basis that allows ordinary players to attain extraordinary results.

The Wellington Lions team exhibited this spirit in winning the 2000 NPC championship against Canterbury. For the last fifteen minutes of the game they were pinned inside their own twenty two against the extraordinary might of the Canterbury team, which couldn't break through to score. It was unprecedented for such a powerful Canterbury side not to be able to score after such a sustained period on attack. The spirit of the Wellingtonians kept them out. Norm Hewitt played on with a broken arm rather than leave the field. It was will power that kept Canterbury out. That's what can happen when the team spirit is so intense.

I witnessed an extraordinary event like that with a team I helped to coach. They were thirteen points down with just on five minutes left to play. They rallied and scored. We didn't know at the time that the forward standing out on the blindside of the ruck was there because he had a broken collarbone and didn't want to leave the field. He created the extra man and scored in the corner, dragging two defenders with him. Our fullback, who had 'frozen' in the first game of the season, converted from the sideline. We had worked to get his confidence back and now it paid off. Back at half way the players were gripped by the inspiration they could win. From the kickoff they repeatedly drove up the middle and through absolute determination forced their way under the posts to win the game with the conversion. It was seeing this unshakeable will power and belief that they could do it that I shall never forget. They knew they could make it happen. This is what grows out of team spirit.

At the core of effective preparation is team cohesion. Team spirit, a bond among team members, strengthens the resolve to play well. Players will be willing to make sacrifices for the betterment of the team. An example of this spirit can be seen in road cycling. Lance Armstrong's Tour de France victories have been achieved through the efforts of team members who have shielded Armstrong and implemented the tactics to get him through to wearing the tour leader's yellow jersey and winning. The coach's goal is to teach players to be unselfish in their commitment to the team. This may require a player to play out of position or to make the plays for others to score.

Team spirit is an aspect that Rod Macqueen developed in his Australian team. This has come about through the emphasis he gave to this aspect of leadership. His approach was far better than the Spartan character of the All Blacks. Little wonder the Australians were so dangerous when just a few points behind towards the end of the game. They could call on that extra human dimension that was in the heart of team. Being able to build and maintain this quality is one of the gifts of coaching.

Leadership style and team spirit

It is the combination of high achievement and encouragement that produces team spirit. A supportive approach can be demanding, as coaches expect players to grow and develop. They give players encouragement and help them to attain higher standards. If they are unable to reach these standards then something has to be done about it, but not in a harsh way. It may be necessary to take a player out of a position if he has not met the required standard. Every support is given to players, but in the end it is necessary for the coach to make a decision. At a conference in America, I met a delegate who was cut from the Miami Dolphins by Coach Don Shula. Shula explained to him why he was not making the cut, made sure he still felt part of the wider Dolphin's family, and did it all with the player's self-esteem intact. It shows why Shula was a coach who inspired loyalty and respect.

It is about having authority and being inclusive. The authority the coach gains comes from a 'psychological contract' with the players. It is the respect and acceptance of the coach's role. I saw a powerful example of this 'psychological contract' one year when we didn't appoint a captain in a secondary school team. When asked who would make the decisions, we gave the vague answer that the player nearest the referee could decide, or the one who was closest to the ball. Within a short time an informal leader had emerged. As the season progressed he developed more authority. It was the 'psychological contract' he had with the team. This is a very effective way of appointing a captain at this level. Usually the teacher makes the choice and the 'new captain' tends to assume a slightly authoritative approach and acts like a prefect. This is the power style which uses the authority of the position to control because of inexperience in a leadership role.

I have continued to use this method of appointing captains. Leaders appointed through this informal process are much more aware of the need to be inclusive. They can, however, make decisions and expect others to follow. The pattern of leadership that emerges is much more effective. One year we ended up with co-captains. One was very good at reading a game and had a logical approach, while the other was a fiery flanker. The flanker would stir up the 'troops' while the other would comment on how the game was evolving and revise the strategy.

Tapping the motivation of players and building team spirit is essential to eliciting top performance. It is a matter of being absolutely positive. By taking an optimistic but realistic approach that emphasises the excitement and satisfaction of accomplishment, players will be inspired to give their best. Creating that atmosphere taps the will power and a determination inside each player. I first experienced this with my old school in Auckland when I was invited to assist with coaching. They had been promoted to the A grade and their goal was to avoid relegation. When I met them they had already lost their first game. My approach totally changed their expectations. They had to give their best and they gave it. Unexpectedly we won the championship, and then went on to win the following two as well. It was the first year that I look back on with pride, because the championship was achieved through raw courage and determination. Later they evolved more skill as many of the players remained in the team.

On the strength of having discovered a motivational approach that enthused these young players, I wanted to try it on a senior team. The opportunity arose when no-one wanted to coach a Wellington club team that had just been promoted into the senior A competition. We tried to set a realistic target which was to either make the top six or win fifty percent of our games. After a discussion on which choice we should make, someone worked out that if we won fifty percent of our games we would be in the top six playoff. We managed to win half our games and came sixth equal. The interesting thing about that team was that they never lost a game by *fewer* than fifteen points. We had the worst points for and against record in the competition except the bottom team. If the game was close our determination to win would come through.

Yet with all this success, there were some that didn't like the approach I had to coaching and motivating players. For most of the team it was so enlightening they responded well. For the high-power-oriented players it was not what they wanted or appreciated. They responded better to the hard taskmaster approach. The next year I didn't coach them again. Half of the players from the season before were unable to make the team – the club attracted a whole bunch of new talented players because they were an 'established' senior side. By the end of that second season they were last in the division. It was team spirit that had carried them through the previous year, and without that they were a second-division side.

Power-oriented individuals can be very divisive and are at their best criticising and causing trouble. They can be disruptive. Often they are indirect in the way they undermine the team. Their criticism is usually not constructive. Competitive power-oriented players need a firm hand to control them. To some extent, they respect such treatment. Once I was coaching a team with several 'power types' and they were against my methods of coaching. At one practice, I introduced 'the hill' and gave them a bit of abuse because they hadn't played well. Afterwards the three came up to me and said it was the best practice all season. That is what they wanted from a coach. I learned to give them a bit of verbal abuse at other practices and they thought that was OK.

Over the years I have mainly helped out at secondary school level with my own sons, and helped teachers with some other teams – particularly John, my brother, who was a teacher. He helped to refine some of the concepts that I have developed. We found that, regardless of the lack of talent, we could always get the team half way up the competition ladder by tapping players' motivation to perform well. These were B teams that we put in the A competition. We would rather come up against the best and lose than be in an easicr grade. We also had an enviable record for winning championships. We would not, however, let the boys talk about championship titles. There was enough challenge in the next game without being preoccupied about two points in the championship table. When they experience the intensity and drama of rugby the way we coached, the players got enough thrills and satisfaction regardless of the outcome. Of course our approach was more likely to result in superior performance and winning. Good sportsmanship in losing was a prerequisite for being in any of our teams. As has already been said, when you have done your best there is no reason to be disappointed. In fact, after some great struggles where we gave our best and lost, we have been more proud than when we did win. I have seen players exhausted and proud of themselves because they tapped into a pride inside themselves which, as Lou Holtz said, eschewed mediocrity.

A couple of dramatic cases where I have helped teams on a one-off basis to achieve extraordinary results also serve as examples of the effectiveness of the motivational approach. Usually I avoided such situations as it takes a little time to develop the attitudes I want in players. In Rotorua, I was doing consulting work with a forestry group once and they invited me along as guest coach of their senior club team. I went through my routine of points, variation and gaining the initiative. They expressed appreciation and politely thanked me. This team had always been in the bottom of the competition and true to form lost their next two games. I had the opportunity to be back in Rotorua a couple of weeks later and took umbrage that my effect had been negligible. We had a team meeting on a non-practice night. One of the team members didn't attend as he was against the idea of being harangued in an aggressive team talk. That was what he expected. Instead we covered what the real essence of the game of rugby was all about. It meant giving their best. Something that each player had to do was dig down deep inside and find in himself the will power to be motivated beyond his present level of performance. This meant they needed to think beyond what they thought was possible. It was a commitment that they had to silently make to themselves and their team mates – a powerful commitment

On Saturday the game was a total contrast in performance to anything that the team had ever experienced before. Earlier they had told me that they weren't that big. I was looking at tall strapping young men and told them so – they were big. When I saw the St Michael's team I understood why they thought they were small. St Michael's were massive. Our team played beyond themselves. It was a game for their club to be proud of, and even the St Michael's coach joined me on the sideline saying how great it was to see how committed our team was and how well they were performing. He couldn't help but admire the spirit of Eastern, whom I was helping. In fact, he was almost cheering for us because he thought it so good to see a team that had been bottom for so long performing extraordinarily well – a true sportsman who could acknowledge the merit of the other side. We have yet to see an All Black coach applaud a great try by the opposition.

At half-time the captain of our side was ecstatic about the team effort, 'This is the sort of team that I want to be playing for.' The spirit and commitment they were making to one another and the determination it engendered enthralled them. This team went on to win the remaining games in the round and were only defeated in the final. I went back to help them for the final at the suggestion of the player who didn't attend the first team talk! Unfortunately my lack of appreciation at that time of what was needed for finals preparation meant I didn't quite get the best out of the team.

Another engagement that left an impression on me was when I helped a Maori rugby league team in Hawke's Bay. They were in the semi-finals, up against a side that they had not beaten in ten years. I plotted with them about how they were going to get the initiative and score points. They won that game, and then had to prepare for the final. By this time I knew more about preparing for finals. We kept the team relatively relaxed and focused. In the dressing room before the match we decided that we would not give a team talk. The dressing room got quieter and quieter until five minutes before the game it was totally silent. They just looked at each other. This was their hapu (tribe). The atmosphere was immensely powerful. The game was virtually won before they went out of the dressing room door.

These examples highlight the impact of team spirit on performance. Usually team spirit isn't developed as a result of a one-off session but builds over time. The Eastern team did have me to an earlier practice and the result was inconclusive, but in that second session something dramatic was captured. Somehow it tapped the core values of achievement and affiliation. These motives created the desire to excel, combined with a commitment to others in the team. It was a deeper intrinsic desire that drove their performance. The inspiration came from within and was mystically shared with others to create a powerful dynamic in the team. For those who have experienced it, no explanation is necessary; for those who have not experienced it, no explanation is possible.

Players do respond to leadership, and once their commitment has been gained they will show courage and determination to achieve the objectives that have been set. This dedication prepares them to make the sacrifices necessary to compete and not yield. They will not settle for anything but their best. It is an extraordinary quality we all possess. In watching the emergence of such motivation in teams over the years I am reminded of the painting by Michelangelo in the Sistine Chapel. God is reaching out to man but their fingers don't quite meet. Somehow something jumps across that gap like an electron jumping a neural junction in the brain and firing the person with a new sense of purpose.

The explanation that I have come up with is that creating the setting through leadership, and being able to espouse the values underlying team spirit, produces a response in players that harnesses the noble qualities we are after. Encouragement and personal interest in players is also involved. Besides the emotional appeal to players, understanding and directing them towards achievement values sets them on a mission of self discovery. They confront the will within themselves to want to succeed. This can be both a frightening and an inspiring experience. To dare to excel is to risk failure. It means struggling and facing setbacks. Players will experience exhilaration and happiness. While it can be experienced more acutely in sport, it is a self-sustaining drive that applies to all aspects of life. That is why coaching is also a form of teaching. We are teaching players to harness the finest qualities they possess.

Optimism allows individuals and teams to dare to achieve great things. It is the faith that leads to achievement, and nothing can be done without such faith and confidence. Such qualities cannot be developed in ease and quiet. They are achieved only through experiences of trial and effort. Achieving these qualities is not just a matter of chance. It is a matter of choice. The coach enlists players who are willing to commit to this effort. It is not something we wait for, it needs to be solicited. Within a sporting context, it is the team spirit – shaped by the players' willingness to be committed to the team and give their every effort to attain the goal.

Summary

Team spirit is a quality that shines through in a group that has come together in a way that produces a special sort of team. It is the selfless way players commit to their team and respond to the call for excellence. It is a quality that is elicited by top coaches and is gained through the effective use of leadership strategies. Coaches need to build and reinforce team spirit. It is this quality in a team that produces a passion and purpose in performance that cannot be eclipsed.

Chapter 9

MATCH PLAY

The pressure is on the coach come match play. How the team has been prepared and approaches the game will have a significant influence on their performance. It is not only the culmination of the week's preparation but also the deeper attitudes and beliefs that have been inculcated into the team over time that shine through. Now it is all on the line. How a team plays is a reflection of their coach. The competitiveness of the situation creates anxiety. How coaches handle this will tell a lot about their mental attitude and leadership style. Results do count. However, too much emphasis can be put on the result. The All Blacks are totally despondent if they lose. There is such negativity about losing that fear can grip the players and coaches so that it forms the basis of their motivation. This fear of losing inhibits a team's performance.

Stalin said, 'The masses are ruled by fear.' Franklin D Roosevelt's quote, 'The only thing we have to fear is fear itself,' is in contrast to the Soviet dictator's idea. One society was based on freedom and enterprise and the other on exerting authority and control. The more successful a society, the more it is able to respond to challenge in a confident manner. The historian Arnold Toynbee once said in summing up history, 'Great societies rose and fell by their ability to respond to challenge.' This is the same in a team. It is important that sport reinforces these values. It is the formula for success. What do fear and anxiety have to do with creating excellence? What is sport about if a fear of losing becomes one of the dominant influences in motivating players?

Anxiety interferes with performance

Naturally there will be some anxiety about performance. There is, however, a great deal of difference between anxiety and activation before a game. This is the difference between positive and negative motivation. Activation is feeling built-up and energised. It induces the adrenalin in the system that gives strength and invigorates the mind and body. There still exists a certain level of anxiety that needs to be handled by reinforcing a positive frame of mind. On the one hand players feel the attraction of the coming contest, and on the other a concern about performing well. Sometimes they almost wish they were somewhere else. Motor co-ordination is impaired by stress. It limits the ability to make finely tuned movements or judge what decisions to make. Tension leads to missed passes and mistakes. When players settle down they play better. This often takes place during the first few minutes of a game. The skill of coaching is to have players activated but not to allow anxiety to build and affect their concentration and performance.

Without realising it, coaches often build anxiety and adversely affect the team. Conversely, some coaches are not intense enough so the team lacks the activation to perform at their best. Anxiety reduces the quality of performance. Take the example of Stu Wilson when he first got into the All Blacks. He was known for dropping the ball. Pass it to Stu and he would drop it. He announced that he was not going to be available for the All Blacks. Two All Black friends got with him, Graham Mourie and Mark Sayers, and helped him to come to terms with the pressure of playing at international level. He then announced that he would be available for selection, and in his mind it didn't matter if he got dropped. From there he went on to become the highest try-scoring All Black.

In a television documentary about coaching the North Harbour NPC team, one of the coaches before the game goaded players about what the opposition were going to do to them – how the opposition was going to 'get stuck into them' – as if this was a way of rousing their motivation. All it would do would be to subtly raise anxiety and sow seeds of defeat in their minds. It was undermining their confidence. To someone high on power it seems a plausible action, as arousing fear is seen as a motivator!

Aggression in sport

Another approach some coaches use is frustration/aggression motivation. They psychologically prod players to frustrate and evoke aggressive responses from them so they become angry, and that anger is then focused on the opposition. Fred Allen used this tactic. He would work players up in his pep talks and they became so charged up that these feelings were transferred to the game. To a large extent, players, like Wilson Whineray who played under Allen, knew it was a technique and never let the negativity get to them.

This frustration/aggression approach has adverse consequences because players take out their aggression on the opposition. It leads to foul play and breaking the rules. The underlying motive is to want to fight and injure an opposition player. The coach is usually horrified with this effect without realising that he was inciting such behaviour. It is not that he intends players to act that way, but he sets the psychological conditions for it to happen. This is an abuse of motivational strategies. In the end it does interfere with players' focus on the game. When you see players primed this way they usually get penalised and cost their team points. It is particularly destructive when such methods are used with players who are prone to anger and aggression.

Aggression does play a part in sport but there is a need to appreciate the acceptable bounds of such emotion. There are two types of aggression. The first is reactive aggression. This evokes anger and the urge to want to strike a player. It is focused on the individual and can be irrational. The purpose is to destroy, inflict punishment on or hurt another player. Reactive aggression is aroused through the tactics already outlined. It evokes direct aggression against the opposition. It encourages players to literally go out and attack the opposition. Before rugby was televised, tactics to try to intimidate the opposition were almost condoned. They still happen today. The French have eye-gouged, put the boot in and ripped at the testicles of players. Such acts are designed to upset and intimidate.

When power motives become excessive they can result in a level of aggression that is beyond the bounds of sportsmanship – like wanting to 'get' the opposition. Such players become agitated and vent their anger at the opposition rather than concentrating on playing the game. They are bent on inflicting damage on their opponent as an end in itself. This anger and hostility does not have a place in sport. Players with these attitudes want to intimidate by fair or foul means. The use of such means leads to violence. Vengefulness comes into play. It does have the effect of intimidating the opposition. Players can accumulate a certain amount of prestige and status by this behaviour. As one player like this said, 'Would you rather have me on your side than against you.' There is a tendency for them to justify their unacceptable behaviour as being good for the team. I have known coaches to quietly condone such behaviour because it could make a difference in getting on top of the opposition.

Reactive aggressive emotions arouse hatred. Building an intense dislike of the opposition can evoke it. This can be done by letting it be known that the opposition has been insulting your players, or by building the competitive nature of the conflict so 'it is either them or us who will survive'. Some coaches actually think this is what psychological techniques are all about. They appeal to the primordial motives that are in all of us. It starts to give one an understanding of why war crimes are committed. The belief that there needs to be more 'mongrel' conjures up images of being a vicious dog. This may not be what is intended but it is easily misconstrued. This is taking it too far and being too reactionary – evoking hatred of and aggression against the opposition. Rugby is a thinking game that requires organisation and discipline. It is a bit like having the Mongrel Mob up against the SAS – who would you back?

There needs to be an accepted standard of behaviour. Warfare was once conducted with such understanding. Once Lord Nelson boarded a ship and found himself surrounded, as the enemy had not surrendered. When the situation was made clear, he was escorted to the side and transferred back to his ship. After further engagement the enemy surrendered and he re-boarded to relieve them of their command.

Players like Norm Hewitt started pouring their anger into rugby. Hewitt believed that is what gave him the edge in performance. When he was on the field he would look at the opposition and think, 'I'm going to break the guy's neck, maim him, or do something that is going to be really damaging.' That was his mentality. He accused Sean Fitzpatrick, 'the king of sledging', of such a hurtful comment that he sought revenge. Hewitt says, 'It took me five years to draw blood from him but I put stitches in his face.'[1] Richard Loe also had reactive aggressive tendencies, using eye gouging and his elbow to inflict damage on players. This behaviour does not have a place in sport, yet it is tolerated and, strangely, admired in an obscure sort of way. This is because deep down inside all of us, there was some time when we wanted to do something similar, but conscience held us back.

Unfortunately, reactive aggression can be disguised in all sorts of comments. Even when the coach doesn't intend to exhort players to such behaviour, language like 'Hit him,' 'Belt the hell out of them,' 'Fight' and 'Get stuck into them' can unintentionally arouse reactive aggression in players. Rugby is a physical game and, as in any contact sport, there is an aggressive element to the game. There needs to be a proper understanding of what the appropriate level is however.

The coach needs to focus on instrumental aggression. This is a form of aggression that is not directed personally at the opposition. In rugby, instrumental aggression could be demonstrated by a determination to break through the tackle of a defender to get to the line and score. In other words, the aggression is instrumental to the task and not directed at the person. Instrumental aggression is aggressive behaviour that has the purpose of achieving some goal. The purpose of reactive aggression is to directly injure or hurt another player. Instrumental aggression is about courage, fearlessness and tenacity to achieve a goal. It is aggression that is within the context of the game and sportsmanship. Instrumentally aggressive players can leave their aggression on the field. In other areas of their lives they do not exhibit such aggressive behaviour unless it is necessary in a particular situation. They know how to assert themselves without getting upset or angry. The reactive aggressive approach is often associated with players who are angry and maladjusted off the field.

When coaches excite reactive aggression, players often feel caught in an emotional conundrum. They feel inhibited about using reactive aggression. The naturally reactive aggressive player will respond to the coach who resorts to suggesting that other players be harmed physically. A normally adjusted player will feel some conflict about the coach exciting them to such behaviour. It is in conflict with their consciences. They usually know to water down what the coach is saying. Many players find themselves with conflicting emotions about aggression. Emphasising instrumental aggression removes the dilemma. Physical contact is part of the game of rugby, and being physically assertive is important in gaining the initiative. Taking the physical encounter to the opposition helps a team to get the psychological edge. Psychological ascendancy and gaining the initiative includes the physical aspects of the game as well as in the patterns of play. This is why players need to be physically well conditioned and mentally tough.

Toughness isn't about being a bully. It is about character and determination. It is about focusing on the game and what is required to attack and defend. It is about winning rucks, getting ball turnover, tackling and scoring tries. Passion and effort are directed at playing the game in a physically robust way within the rules. Someone who exemplified this was Michael Jones, who was known for his strong tackling. Francois Pienaar said, 'For a Christian, Michael Jones tackles very hard.' His great reply was, 'It is better to give than receive.' Jones was never penalised for foul play. He didn't hate the opposition. He always had a courteous manner and respect for other players. That is the attitude that needs to be engendered in players.

Achievement focus

Coaches need to use non-judgemental language, ways of saying things that concentrate on inspiring players without evoking reactive aggression. The language that is used should not carry negative connotations of aggression against other people. The images that are evoked should create a mindset in players that is positive. Coaches should be inspiring players to do their best, identifying the tasks they have to perform and clarifying how they have to be done. This might require developing dominance in the forwards. That would entail the coach telling players about being first to the breakdown, driving forward play, winning rucks and being fast up in defence and tackling. All this requires physical courage and determination. It is requires good tackling, but not 'big hits.' Interestingly enough, this type of mental conditioning leads to a more vigorous style of play because players feel they are able to be robust – since they remain within the rules of fair play.

The anxiety players experience is mainly caused by a concern about how they will perform and that they will look bad if they do something wrong. What is at stake is their sense of self-esteem and worth as a person. Players who have a positive view of themselves handle this better. They have usually received positive messages about themselves and do not feel threatened in a sporting conflict. Many actually thrive on the competitiveness of the situation. They see the opposition as challenging them to greater performance rather than as a threat. Others have to overcome negative messages in their heads and their concern about failure. This can lead to struggling with a lack of confidence in their own ability. Reinforcing achievement values helps them to overcome the tendency to have such self-defeating thoughts. By creating a positive atmosphere in the team, the coach reduces the 'threat' that is inherent in pre-match nerves.

My nephew, who won the New Zealand decathlon championship, exemplified this attitude. When he was a junior, he was in the Australian championships and was equal with the Australian junior champion on points. In the hurdles event the Australian fell and lost valuable time and points. There was only the 1500 metres to go and Sean's response was one of disappointment. 'That guy was pushing me through to my best times and he was a better middle distance runner than me, so I would have had to really compete in that race.' Now there was less competition he virtually had the decathlon won. 'If he hadn't fallen it would have ended up that I would have had to get one of my best times in the 1500 and that would have given me my highest score for any decathlon.' He wanted to win, but he was also inspired by striving for excellence.

Match preparation

Before a match, keep emphasising the game plan and how to deal with the opposition's strengths and weaknesses. Achievement-oriented coaches use good analytical skills to figure out and plan strategies carefully. Attacking the weaknesses in the opposition is like using a hammer against a brick wall. It means: Keep hammering at the weak brick until it crumbles and the wall starts to fall in on itself. By directing some of the play at the weak points in the opposition, an uncertainty is created that demolishes their confidence and they can cave in like the wall. In doing this there is also the need to remind the team to play their game, gain the initiative, and focus on what is expected of them. This means focusing on what they are going to do and not on their opposition. In the build up to a game, keep emphasising the standards they are trying to achieve, and what they must do to achieve them.

While the game is about wanting to win, the team will get satisfaction from giving their best. The most important message is points, points and more points! Emphasise that 'we can out-score the opposition.' The game is about scoring points. To highlight this spirit, I gave a cup to be played among sister colleges. It was to be awarded to the team that scored the best try in the game. This changes the emphasis of the play. It makes the game a celebration of the joy of rugby. Even when the strengths of the two sides are disproportionate, the underdogs are still trying to pull off a great try and win the trophy.

General Patton said, 'Defeat is only in the mind and that only happens when you say that you are defeated.'[2] Knowing you did your best means that in spirit you are never defeated. Your head can be held high and there is pride in having competed. I have dealt many situations like this – where there was real pride at having strived for excellence – and felt so proud of the players. Build the will to win. This is done by emphasising determination, and focusing on task mastery. The closer to the game, the more players should concentrate on *how to win* and not on *winning* itself. Give positive reassurance. It is by what they do right, not what they do wrong, that you should judge their performance. This creates a far more positively charged atmosphere. The interesting thing is that by removing the anxiety about doing something wrong, fewer mistakes actually occur. I have seen teams go out and score some great tries when they have this attitude. When supporters on the sideline ask how I trained them to do that I have to admit, 'It's the first time I've seen that as well.' Releasing their anxiety about failure and increasing their enthusiasm to do things right creates a whole new dimension in team performance. Such instruction is paramount for outstanding performance. It is important that the coach live up to that dictum. Believe me, at junior level especially, it transforms their approach to the game. Trying to avoid mistakes makes players cautious and tentative. It is like being on the high wire and looking down – a sure way to lose confidence and fall.

Team cohesion

Team cohesion is one of the prime factors that influences match play. Cohesion is a matter of being constantly aware of the group dynamics and creating the right kind of atmosphere during the build up for a game. What top teams have in common is the willingness to serve the greater good of the team. This lead comes from the coach. There should always be optimism about what can be accomplished. At the heart of true cohesion is selflessness and a commitment to the others in the team and the goals the team is trying to achieve. Forging a high degree of unity builds championship teams. The senior players and the captain are commissioned with this responsibility, as well as the coach. The coach needs to take time with these players to discuss how to raise the level of play of their team-mates. They do this by disregarding their own interests for the betterment of the team.

Researchers studying bravery in warfare wanted to find out why some combat units stood and fought while others tended to abandon fire-fights. Initial contact with the enemy required platoons to open fire immediately rather than dive for cover. The aim was to keep the enemy pinned down rather than themselves. Maintaining fire meant that the soldiers were exposed to the enemy. When the whole platoon maintained their firepower everyone was equally exposed to the danger of being shot. If, however, a number went to ground and did not shoot at the enemy, then those who remained and continued with the supressing fire were more vulnerable. The researchers found there were particular units which had a higher 'trigger pulling' ratio when first engaging in combat. They found that the motive to stand and fight among these men wasn't caused by fear or patriotic reasons, but because they didn't want to let their mates down. The cohesion and commitment to one another was what inspired bravery.

It may not be possible to get every player to subscribe to this philosophy of unselfishness. Such notions could be outside their experience and harder to induce. However, I believe that most who play team sports are attracted to the game because they enjoy the comradeship of other players. With the right encouragement they will give their all for the team. The coach needs to build this value in the nucleus of the team and create positive attitudes. Rituals and affirmations about team commitment reinforce the message and also promote unity and determination in players before the game. All this strengthens the bond between players and the purpose of their unity. The outcome is that they play with courage and are far more fearless.

Building team cohesion produces group-induced aggression. As a team becomes more unified and members have closer emotional ties, the determination to exert themselves and put their bodies on the line for the team becomes stronger. The messages around instrumental aggression have more meaning. Often what happens is that an 'average player' picks up on these messages about maximising physical contact and acts more aggressively. This determination and example of instrumentally aggressive behaviour seems to fire up other members, particularly in the forward pack.

It inspires others to lift their game and unleashes a level of effort that is usually buried inside. It's great to play in a team when the spirit is up and there is a sense of inspiration and determination. Experiencing such emotion is exhilarating and character building.

The coach needs to get players to focus on the game plan. A team will have developed a pattern of play that has been building up throughout the pre-season and early games. This is based on the style of play the coach wants to encourage, working it around the skills of the players. The game plan essentially takes into account the qualities of the opposition's strengths and weaknesses. At lower levels, not that much is usually known about the opposition and the aim is to gain the initiative and stick to the pattern of play the team has developed. Where more analysis of the opposition can be done, the game plan needs to highlight how to counter the opposition's play. Video analysis provides valuable insight into the moves and play of the opposition and has become a major tool at top levels.

The game plan should not divorce itself from the pattern that is the normal style for the team. It becomes unsettling if players find that they are drastically changing their pattern, and it leads to a lack of co-ordination and teamwork. Goals can be set for the team and for individuals. They can range from the number of tackles a player aims to make, to the percentage of possession the team should aim for and the range of moves the coach wants executed. This keeps players focusing on what they are going to do rather than worrying about the opposition.

Laurie Mains conceived a game plan to win the World Cup by developing a pattern of play that used the forwards to sprint up the middle. Other teams have now picked up on the pattern of having runners. At the time it added a new dimension to the game. It countered a defence that spread too wide. Now, with the five-second rule for mauls, game plans need to be adjusted from just running the ball up. The Lions could have won the test series in Australia if they had concentrated on driving the mauls with their big forwards. The Australian defence was geared to dealing with runners and had difficulty dealing with driving mauls.

The different tactics employed can lead to different selections of players. Driving mauls need bigger and heavier forwards and less emphasis on speed is needed. A way of countering the driving maul could be to play a faster game and run the heavier opposition forwards all over the paddock. It would then become a matter of who could get the initiative and dominate play. Within the range of these two options are a number of other patterns.

Build up to the game

The build up to the game usually follows a fairly set pattern. Practices are based on the game plan. The psychological preparedness of the team needs to be judged. If the players appear a little jaded it may pay to have a less intense practice and more variation of drills to make it fun. At other times the practice can be more intense and focused. One of the best tactics I have found when playing against traditional rivals is to build the delight in playing in such a game and remind players how it is always an exciting contest. This does not mean seeing the opposition as someone who has to be 'beaten', 'crushed' or 'defeated'. This aggressive view is becoming more prevalent in the marketing of sports contests and distorts attitudes to the game. It inhibits the freer expression of players. Build into them a sense of excitement and an enjoyment of the game and a higher level of performance will result. Keep in mind Eric Watson's comment – he is one of New Zealand's most successful entrepreneurs and revived the Warriors franchise – 'It can all be too serious – far too serious. It's only money'. We should keep in mind that rugby is only a game.

The build-up on the day of the match will vary according to the level being played. For club teams there is usually a Thursday night after-practice session, outlining thoughts and a review of the game plan. For school teams this may not be necessary but I have always found a Friday lunchtime meeting helpful to gain focus, and players respond well to the talk. It is lower-keyed than a team talk just before the match. It should be used to reiterate the achievement values being developed in the team, commitment to the team, and provide reassurance to players. This assurance is important. Jeff Wilson noticed when his father died that there was a gap, a loss of support. The emphasis should be on giving one's best. The attitudes being promoted are lessons for life and draw on that inner quality of fortitude.

Individual preparation for a game varies according to different personalities and each players' personal motivation. Much of sport psychology has been focused on this aspect. It is more applicable to top athletes who compete in the Olympic Games than to rugby players who play week after week. Still, some lessons can be learned. Grant Fox advocates visualisation techniques and he obviously finds them useful. This requires you to conceptualise in your head the way you are going to play and the different situations that you might find yourself in during a game. This visualisation should always be positive. When Alison Rowe won the New York marathon, she imagined herself at every stage of the race and then went out and did it. For those high on achievement this is naturally part of the thinking process. To artificially take the technique and apply it does not have the same impact. Achievers are able to imagine themselves being successful and want the opportunity to take risks and succeed.

Relaxation and sound sleep are a part of good preparation. This is particularly important around finals or a big game. Diet also affects players. Colin Meads still thinks there is nothing wrong with a big steak before a game, but it is carbohydrates that provide energy. Protein is for muscle repair and useful after the game. Many players are also unsure about how much fluid to drink. Rugby is a game that quickly dehydrates players and they need to compensate with fluid intake. Sports drinks help at half-time and after the game. They quickly replace electrolytes and restore the body's balance. Carbohydrates are also necessary. There is a half-hour window of opportunity after a game to have carbohydrates, or recovery will take a lot longer. In that time the body readily absorbs the sustenance. This preparation and after-match nutrition and hydration keep players tuned-up to achieve their best.

Team talks

Team talks also influence performance. They set the tone of play expected of players. It is possible to talk up a side. There is a definite relationship between the achievement values of the coach and how these attitudes are translated into team performance. A study in Michigan of high school football teams found a perfect correlation between the level of achievement measured in the coach and how the team performed in the championship. In other words, the higher the coach was in terms of achievement values the better the team result. Across twelve teams, the coaches' level of achievement ranked the same as where their teams came in the competition. This is dynamite information and brings home the impact of these values on performance.

Team talks are usually more dramatic earlier in a season as attitudes are forming. By the end of a season the thinking that is in place needs less reinforcement as the team has already come together and fewer words are necessary. The power of team talks has been underestimated in recent times. It may be that they were seen as hype and not connected with reality, or coaches were not articulate enough. As has been said, many of those high on achievement can't explain what it is, so how can they consciously instil this attitude in others. Team talks, which build achievement attitudes, make a difference. When the game gets to a crucial stage these attitudes lift performance. Tad Baldwin's articulate team talks were part of the reason the Tall Blacks played so well at the World Basketball Games.

For coaches who don't have achievement values, the less said before a game, the better. The coach can work up an intensity and purpose in the team, not just through the words he uses in the team talk but by quietly going around the players and commenting. During this preparation emphasis is placed on the game plan, teamwork and points, points and more points. The smell of liniment creates an atmosphere in the dressing room. I favour staying in the dressing room until just before the start of the match rather than having too much time out on the field. This adds to the intensity. It may pay for the backs to be less tense before the game as they have to execute finely tuned skills, whereas the forwards are going into a very vigorous physical encounter straight from the kick-off and need that intensity.

Take some of Shakespeare's great lines as examples of team

talks. In *Henry V* he rallies his troops, 'Once more unto the breach, dear friends, once more.' And before they charge he says, 'Stiffen the sinews, conjure up the blood, disguise fair nature with hard-favoured rage. Now set the teeth, follow your spirit; and upon this charge cry – God for Harry! England! – and Saint George!' Again, before the battle of Agincourt, outnumbered 600 against 20,000, Henry says, 'We few, we happy few, we band of brothers: for he today who sheds his blood with me shall be my brother.' After this great speech, he won. He did have the longbow, which was a new invention in warfare. Archers could shoot eleven rounds a minute, with four or five arrows in the air at one time so they rained down on the French. The long bow had such force it would penetrate armour. Besides this innovation, Henry also chose the battlefield carefully. It was hemmed in on both sides by woods, making a narrow approach for the French. This concentrated their force and made them susceptible to the archers. All of this shows a good use of tactics, motivational speech and innovation.

The captain plays a key role in maintaining the teams focus and bringing the players together before the game. The huddle before they go out is part of the ritual that binds the team together. It is a very powerful experience. It seems that rugby engenders the feeling of unity more strongly than other sports. It is the combination of physical demand, the high level of teamwork required and identification with each other that makes it so intense. This experience is very profound and gives a great deal of support to each member of the team. It is something that really needs to be experienced in order to be understood.

At half-time

At half-time, the talk should be quick and concise. Solicit any relevant information from players. This should not be a general discussion as there won't be time. The coach should summarise the play in the first half. It is important to identify who has the initiative, or how it has swung between the teams and why. It may mean revising the game plan if the initial plan is not working out. It is not really a time for emotional appeals as players have expended so much physical energy that they will not be keyed up for that type of appeal, though there is still a need to convey a sense of urgency and purpose. The players must know what they have to do in the second half in order to win. It is not a time to talk about techniques. Often half-time talks are just a coaching session on tackling or lineout drills and not about the flow of play, who has the initiative and what to do in the second half. Coaching techniques can be left to the next practice.

If the team isn't performing well, it is necessary to tell them that they are not playing to the best of their ability and it is not good enough. There may also be a need to revisit the basics if they aren't working. These have to be right in order to build your game. The focus should be on the run of play, tactics and the game plan. There is a need to look at what moves have worked and what plays they should make. The speech needs to be positive overall. The coach in this situation is operating in an authoritarian/democratic style. Communication needs to be honest and direct. This is consistent with high achievement behaviour, as the situation does not allow for much participation. After the game and at the next practice there will be time for everyone to comment and give their analysis.

If the team does not play well the coach needs to keep his emotions in check. It doesn't serve any purpose to get angry with them. While there is emotion in such situations, it should be about the performance and not directed personally. Such comments can upset players if they take them personally and this will affect their confidence. Slang and swearing should be used sparingly because they are imprecise and will usually not convey the coach's real meaning. It is important to set a realistic goal if you think you can't beat the opposition. It is unrealistic to make the team go for impossible goals and will only spell failure. If my team were thirty points down at half-time and hadn't scored, I would tell them to never give in and set a target of two tries in the second half. It is just hype to keep talking about winning when that far behind. I wouldn't actually say we couldn't win. If the team found that they were five points behind with ten minutes to go, then they would be back in the game.

After the game

After the match, be positive no matter what the result. When you win it doesn't pay to be boastful and there is a need to be graceful in accepting defeat. My father always said, 'Anyone can laugh when they win, it takes a good sport to laugh when he loses.' Sportsmanship is the key component of the coach's approach during and after the game. After the game, review what went well. Problems can be dealt with later in a team session or at the next practice. Recognising what went well and building on it rather than concentrating too much on mistakes engenders progress. In the section on leadership, it was highlighted that one of the key strategies that leaders use to create excellence is to notice when things are done well. It is not only the result that counts but how the team plays.

Ross Cooper, when achieving good results with Counties, encountered one game where the team played poorly and missed at least six scoring opportunities. The next practice was televised, showing him saying to the team, 'Great counter attack, good support and excellent how you found the gap; as for the last pass . . . better we don't talk about that.' There was a bit of a nervous laugh. Cooper knew that the players didn't need reminding. There is a need to recognise where things don't go right, but it needs to be done in a constructive manner. The whole thrust should be towards what was done right.

Remember that achievement is about attraction toward success. Look at after-match comments from captains and they are full of what went wrong and the need to work on mistakes. The emphasis is all-wrong. Remember points, points, and more points is about no-mistake rugby for two minutes. In that time four tries could be scored. That would gain bonus points in the Super Twelve Competition. The after-match TV reviews with both captains should be about the highlights of the game. That would then kindle the spirit of enterprise and adventure. Instead I have heard All Blacks saying on television that they are 'gutted', 'shattered' and 'devastated' by a loss. I would rebuke schoolboys for saying such things after a game, yet here are their role models acting like spoilt adolescents. Rugby needs to be presented in an achievement context. It unleashes a whole different attitude to the game. At times, our role models aren't doing it right.

A tradition after the game is to award a 'Player of the Day Award.' When the media do this for top teams it is not taken too seriously. At junior levels it is quite counter productive. I have seen the player of the day announced and seen the disappointment in a number of others. Their shoulders go down. What has just happened is a highly competitive episode. Players are now compared against one another and the emphasis is removed from playing for the team. I expect everyone to play to the best of their ability. Giving an award to one player is sending out a message that is completely counter to that concept. Sean Fitzpatrick's view is that the player of the day isn't real. He says, 'It goes to the glamour players like Kirwan on the wing.' He realised that he sometimes got the player of the day award. He gave some thought about how he managed to get it. Then he realised. 'I go and stand out on the wing and they pass me the ball to score a try.'

Analyse the game

After the game, it is time to celebrate and socialise. This aspect of team sport lies at the heart of New Zealand rugby. It is not a time to be serious. That happens at the next team session. It is then important to review if the team played up to the standards they set themselves. Achievement is about competing against one's own standards. These standards need to be explicit so players know what is expected and how to get there. The team reviews their play and examines what worked and what didn't work. As has already been said, the emphasis should be on looking at what was done right and how to get more things going right. Often, what worked is taken for granted. When you do this you miss the opportunity to build on the excellence that has been achieved. For example, examine how the tries were scored. Often they start from something like a turnover. Emphasise the work of the forward who got to the breakdown first. Other factors are also recognised and this makes players sharper and more able to take advantage of these opportunities in the future.

Analysis of what didn't work should be devoid of blame,

otherwise players become defensive. For example, one of my players ran back from a ruck and tried to take a high ball over his shoulder close to our line but it bobbled out of his hands. From the ensuing maul the opposition scored. On other occasions he had done this successfully. I reinforced the fact that he was taking responsibility rather than letting someone else take the ball. This time it didn't work but that sort of play is what I want to see. It is a matter of being able to give an accurate and honest assessment of what happened and looking for ways to improve that will make the difference. It is important to learn from mistakes rather than to be defensive. This means staying problem-centred. We need to look beyond the obvious. Good analysis comes through thinking about cause and effect, otherwise you end up dealing with symptoms rather than the real problems. A healthy self-regard means that participants are able to deal with issues in a non-defensive way. If anxiety arises, it gets in the way of good analysis and the opportunity to examine and improve performance is missed.

Too many people on the sideline look for mistakes. Once I was at a club game and the person behind me continually criticised the first five, who wasn't having a great game. In frustration I turned to him and asked who was playing well. He didn't know. A little later he tapped me on the shoulder and pointed out a young lock who was giving his all in the lineouts. He told me years later that that exchange transformed the way he watched a game. Incidentally, the first five was All Black Herewini and towards the end of the game he pulled off a spectacular try to win the game. My advice is that if you want to enjoy a game of rugby look for the players playing their best.

Giving positive feedback sets achievement values in the minds of the players far more firmly than chastising them for mistakes. When goals are set they should stretch the abilities of the players as individuals and as a team. Hence, one would expect that not all the goals would be achieved. However, at least seventy five percent of the should be achieved. This means a certain number of goals won't be met. If the emphasis is put on the goals that are not met, the temptation is for players to want to lower the goals so they are all achieved. Review sessions have to be characterised by a lot of cause and effect thinking so players can note where their effort makes a difference.

Each player should be compared against his own standards. This means that a top player may get more critical comments even though he has played better than others in the team. Once I had a top player complain about the low rating of his performance. I asked him if he want be compared with the average performance or with what he was capable of achieving. His answer was he wanted to be assessed against the standard he was capable of achieving. This was a part of what Border did to raise the performance of the Australian cricket team. In the end, the goal has less to do with winning or losing than improving performance. This is where teams fool themselves. Because they are winning they misread the standard they are playing to and don't improve. This kind of thinking will count against them in championship playoffs.

Summary

This chapter has translated the concepts of aggression, power, competitive and achievement values into pre-match, match and after-match approaches. It shows how to use achievement values in these situations. Incorporated in this chapter are earlier chapters dealing with strategy, motivation, leadership and training. The match approach concerns the overall team dynamics that help to gain the psychological edge.

---

1. Michael Laws, *Gladiator – The Norm Hewitt Story*
2. Alan Axelrod, *Patton On Leadership*

EPILOGUE

The introduction of professionalism is changing the nature of the game. Tony O'Reilly, the great Lions winger and international businessman, believes there is a need to preserve the culture and the soul of the game. Corporatisation has shifted the balance to commercialism. 'It needs to be a game we can all play, and enjoy watching.' He believes the unions, players and clubs need to assert themselves to this end.

Reality says that we must now deal with coaching in a professional environment and also maintain our enthusiasm for the game as a participative sport. To achieve this it may be necessary to separate amateur and professional players. Amateur rugby needs to be centred on clubs, tertiary institutions and schools. Strict amateur rules should be followed to maintain the spirit of the game.

There needs to be a strategy that gets rugby into the tertiary institutes. In America, all college/university players in basketball and football teams are amateur. All they can receive is an educational scholarship to the institution. This would be fees, accomodation and a small grant for living expenses. It is only when they graduate that they are eligible to be drafted into the professional ranks. We need to strengthen this level of participation. It would mean that before players became professional they would undertake tertiary studies. This would mean that when their sporting careers finished they would have qualifications to gain employment. We should set this process in place.

Higher educational institutions should become a focus for sport. These would be our universities and technical colleges. In the US, tertiary level games receive nation-wide television coverage. The games are closely followed and tend to be more entertaining than professional games, as the younger players express greater enthusiasm and the games are generally high-scoring. Universities get behind their teams and the games become big events. Everyone has sweatshirts with their college name on them and wears team colours. They identify with their college and their team. Why don't we have the same interest at our institutions?

In our schools there is a need to teach the attitudes, beliefs and values of achievement through participation in sport. Yet many in the teaching profession oppose competitive sports. They feel that such sports engender values that are destructive to the self-esteem of young people. They lack an understanding of achievement motivation. As I have continually reiterated throughout this book, those high on achievement enjoy the spirit of competition as they have learned to handle it properly. They are also the ones who perform better in competitive situations.

It needs to be pointed out that academic achievement does not necessarily relate to the achievement motive. Some pupils perform well at school because of a fear of failure or because their parents are very demanding. That is not motivation through achievement. When a pupil loves the subject and wants to perform well for intrinsic reasons, then the achievement motive has been tapped. Teachers' lack of understanding of the beliefs and underlying values of achievement is certainly costly in terms of developing attitudes in pupils that will make them successful and more able to enjoy life. There is a need for educators to understand the important role sport can play in education. Experiences on the sports field are far more capable of conveying and developing achievement values than any subject in the classroom. Yet this aspect of education is declining and we are losing a potent means of developing constructive attitudes in our young people. This confusion of achievement values with competitive values can be detrimental to understanding the contribution of sport. We have to be careful that the education system is not promoting passive values through their opposition to competitive sports. Success in life has more to do with achievement thinking than it does with academic qualifications.

Sportsmanship needs to be the prerequisite. Club and high school rugby does not have to be as intense about competition as professional rugby. There can be enough rivalry in an inter-school game without worrying about two points in the competition. When coaching at junior levels, I have banned the boys from talking about the competition. During my time at senior level I disliked the talk about two points for a win when there was no satisfaction in the way the game was played. In the end, the championship points look after themselves. The referee who turns up on a Saturday morning and takes two schoolboy games exemplifies the spirit of rugby. He does it for the love of the game and as a service to others.

At club level rugby, while there should be room for a championship round, there should also be an opportunity to play away against 'traditional' rivals. This means arranging games with out-of-town clubs and overnight stays. These are based on enjoyment of the game. The championship round is at the end of the season and by that time players are physically conditioned. Otherwise a more intense need for training means that players pull out because of the time and effort it takes to make such a commitment.

Protocols should be established. Before a game starts there should be three cheers for the other side or even a handshake with the players opposite. The game should be played in a manly spirit. After the game, it should be expected that the host team will offer hospitality and the host player will sort out his opposite number and shout him a drink. What is starting to happen is an increase in hostility towards the opposition and a lack of hospitality. At the professional level some players hardly have a drink with their own team, let alone the opposition. Maori tradition could be called upon in a similar way to a welcome on the marae with a speech from both sides. This mixing of people from all different walks of life is one of the great contributions rugby makes to the New Zealand way of life.

While there is still nostalgia for the old values, we need to move on. One of the distortions of the game has been marketing. This has brought to the game a corporate philosophy and introduced concepts such as calling the All Blacks a 'product.' We have to be careful to keep to the traditions of the game. Advertising agencies find they get more reaction to competitive statements. Promoting test matches as 'payback time,' 'revenge' or 'a grudge match' conjures up competitive/aggressive imagery. It may be good for selling tickets but it is against the spirit of rugby. Fans now boo the opposition and try to put them off whenever they can. Building this dislike of the opposition helps reinforce the marketing of the game. Even Dunedin thinks it smart to call Carisbrook 'the House of Pain'. It sounds a lot more sporting if it is known as 'The Brook'. All this negativity appeals to emotions that are at the lower end of human values.

New Zealand coaches are not good at articulating achievement values. Unlike their counterparts in the United States, who talk about achievement values, our coaches have little formal knowledge of this area of motivation. The coach who talks about and epitomises these values in New Zealand is Tab Baldwin. He is our basketball coach, and he is American. Part of the reason for his expertise in this area is that coaching in the United States is a profession. High schools and colleges have full-time coaches. Our club coaches come from a variety of backgrounds and have not been exposed to sport psychology and, in particular, the concepts of achievement. Quotes from American coaches on achieving excellence are widely used in commerce, education and politics in the US. They contribute to the ideals of that society.

It would be much better if we were able to develop administration, coaching philosophies and marketing campaigns around achievement concepts. This would engender important values in players and the public that would inspire them in other endeavours in life. The game will remain an important part of the social fabric of New Zealand society. It is a game that can build lifelong friendships. No wonder I am still attending rugby reunions twenty-five years later.

BIBLIOGRAPHY

Axelrod, Alan. *Patton On Leadership: Strategic lessons for corporate warfare*, Prentice Hall Press, 1999.

Bennett, Wayne. *Don't Die With The Music In You*, ABC Books, 2002.

Bennis, Warren and Nanus, Burt. *Leaders: Strategies for taking charge*, HarperCollins, 1985.

Cooke, Dr Robert and Lafferty, Dr J Clayton. Human Synergistics thinking and behavioural styles as represented in Life Styles Inventory, Group Styles and Organisational Culture Inventory, Human Synergistics, 1989.

Cooke, Dr Robert. Human Synergistics Leadership/Impact Report (1997) and Organisational Culture Inventory (1989).

Didinger, Ray. *Game Plans For Success: Winning strategies for business and life from 10 top NFL head coaches*, Contemporary Books Inc., Chicago, 1995.

Dwyer, Bob. *The Winning Way*, Rugby Press, New Zealand, 1992.

Gifford, Phil. *Grizz: The Legend*, Rugby Press, New Zealand, 1991.

Gilson, Clive; Pratt, Mike; Roberts, Kevin and Weymes (eds.), *Peak Performance: Business lessons from the world's top sports organisations*, HarperCollinsBusiness, 2000.

Henry, Graham. *The X Factor*, Celebrity Books, 1999.

Hodge, Ken. *Sports Thoughts: Inspiration and motivation for sport*, Reed Books, 2000.

Hodge, Ken and McKenzie, Alex. *Thinking Rugby: Training your mind for peak performance*, Reed Books, 1999.

Holtz, Lou. *Winning Every Day: A game plan for success*, HarperCollins, New York, 1998.

Howitt, Bob and McConnell, Robin. *Laurie Mains*, Rugby Publishing, 1996.

Jackson, Phil and Delehanty, Hugh. *Sacred Hoops: Spiritual lessons of a hardwood warrior*, Hyperion, New York, 1995.

Jaques, Elliott and Clement, Stephen. *Executive Leadership: A practical guide to managing complexity*, Cason Hall & Co., 1991.

Kouses and Posner, *The Leadership Challenge*, Jossey-Bass Inc., 1995.

Laws, Michael. *Gladiator: The Norm Hewitt Story*, Darius Press, 2001.

Macqueen, Rod. *One Step Ahead: On the field and in the boardroom*, Random House, 2001.

McEnroe, John with Kalpan, James. *Serious*, Little, Brown, 2002.

O'Brien, Michael. *Vince: A personal biography of Vince Lombardi,* Quill/William Morrow Publishers, New York, 1987.

Riley, Pat. *The Winner Within: A life plan for team players,* Berkley Publishing Co., New York, 1994.

Romanos, Joseph. *Makers Of Champions: Great NZ coaches,* Mills Publications, 1997.

Shula, Don. *Everyone's A Coach: You can inspire anyone to be a winner,* Zondervan Publishing House, Michigan, 1995.

Thomas, Paul. *Change Of Hart,* Hodder Moa Beckett, 1997.

Verdon, Paul. *The Power Behind The All Blacks: The untold story of the men who coached the All Blacks,* Penguin Books, NZ, 1999.

Walton, Gary. *Beyond Winning: The timeless wisdom of great philosopher coaches,* Leisure Press, Champaign, Illinois, 1992.

Wooden, John and Tobin, Jack. *They Call Me Coach,* Contemporary Books Inc., Chicago, 1988.